M000085956

IF THE ART CAN'T AWE THE CROWD INTO SILENCE

IF THE ART CAN'T SILENCE THE CROWD

IF THE ONLY THING THAT WILL SILENCE THE CROWD

IS THE GALLERY

WHEN THE GALLERY CLOSES

AHSAHTA PRESS
BOISE, IDAHO

2017

THE NEW SERIES
#76

ON A CLEAR DAY

JASMINE DREAME WAGNER

Ahsahta Press, Boise State University, Boise, Idaho 83725-1525
Cover design by Quemadura / book design by Janet Holmes
Cover photograph by Dana Maiden
ahsahtapress.org

LIBRARY OF CONGRESS CATALOGING-IN-PUBLICATION DATA
Names: Wagner, Jasmine Dreame, author.
Title: On a clear day / Jasmine Dreame Wagner.
Description: Boise, Idaho : Ahsahta Press, [2016] | Series: The New Series ; #76
Identifiers: LCCN 2016047221 | ISBN 9781934103692 (softcover) | ISBN
   1934103691 (softcover)
Classification: LCC PS3623.A356304 A6 2017 | DDC 811/.6—dc23
LC record available at https://lccn.loc.gov/2016047221

Thank you to the editors at the following publications for first printing these poems and for allowing them to be reprinted in these pages: *Blackbird*, "Burtynsky's Mines"; *Entropy*, "End Poem"; *Fine Print Paper*, "Bit Rot" and "White Blood Cells"; *New South*, "In the Jewelbox of Childhood," "A Black Gel Pill I Can Take Indefinitely," and "What Comes Next Is, By Definition, Uncertain"; *OmniVerse*: "This is a Private View"; *TYPO*, "Churaevka: A Song"; *Witness*, "A Vivid White Space." "Sunsets" first appeared as a chapbook, *Seven Sunsets*, by The Lettered Streets Press in 2015.

Thank you to my mother, Beth Wagner. Thank you, Joshua Young, Abigail Christian Zimmer, Beya Ozer, and The Lettered Streets Press. Thank you, Christopher Payne, Hilal Omar Al Jamal, Frances Michelle, and Fine Print. Thanks, Gina Abelkop, Raluca Albu, Corey Beasley, Alexis Berthelot, Hannah Berthelot, Adam Clay, Dan Coffey, Joshua Corey, Meghan Maguire Dahn, Christina Dallas, Michelle Detorie, Sean Doyle, Cornelius Eady, George Ferrandi, Michalle Gould, Allison Grillo, Gillian Hamel, Kaylen Hann, Matthew Henricksen, Janet Holmes, Christine Shan Shan Hou, Heba Kadry, David Kirschenbaum, Janice Lee, James Meetze, Lo Kwa Mei-en, David Moore, Rusty Morrison, Kurt Newman, Warren Ng, Kathleen Ossip, Patrick Pritchett, Charlie Rauh, Matt Sargent, Kate Schapira, Jessica Smith, Janaka Stucky, Sondra Sun-Odeon, Mia Theodoratus, Karen Volkman, G.C. Waldrep, Aaron Weber, Jared White, Annie Won, and William Woolfitt. Thanks, Berl's Brooklyn Poetry Shop and The Poetry Project. Thanks, Rick Brooks, for the notebooks. Thanks, Ben Tempchin, Dezbah Stumpff, Roland Ostheim, Aaron Jenks, and everyone at the Dome. Thank you to so many more for teaching me to listen and to see.

FOR MY MOTHER

TABLE OF CONTENTS

"I am legion. The Wolf-Man fascinated
by several wolves watching him."

Gilles Deleuze and Félix Guattari,
A Thousand Plateaus

SNOW

YOU ARE SALT TO ME

As I am salt to you, white dust left after waves have clipped us.

It's difficult to say what I expect to gain from knowing you, as it's impossible to say what I expect to gain from snow. Some new knowledge of the body, an ancient promise, an Egyptology in which I dust the methodology of my own heart's study. I never learn the heart, just the methodology.

I stay up all night listening to you; I listen for you; I stay up all night to make sure the morning will still be there. It is.

A better world begins in the snow of the old one; a better television begins in the snow of the old one; a city under snow is an unauthored work of public art. Snow falls on the pyramids for the first time in 112 years. Celan writes: "Blessed art thou, No One."

Celan is a work of public art. I stand in the snow and think *Celan*. Then I think of Sufjan Stevens. I think of Sufjan's unsung *States*: possibilities? I feel violence in them, the violence of theft, as things that are possible—but kept from us—are stolen.

As there is theft in snow, in poetry. A new snow begins in the theft of the old one. A new poetry begins in the theft of the old one. To move toward poetry as a question itself is a promise of snow: I am compelled to continue beneath it, within it, above it; I am compelled to produce and continue producing tunnels encased in tunnels until I, only a source, am exhausted, am snow.

Celan writes: "the wisdom pit named Never." Sufjan sings: "if you have a father, or if you haven't one." He sings: "What is there to answer if I'm the only one?" Never is never exhausted. An unfathered source is never exhausted, but I am human. I've been named and birthed. I am salt on the world after a long night of snow; I am my expression of formless intensity; I am you; I am you.

SUNSETS

1.1

I read the sun. The subject of the sun is silence.

At sunset, I read the sunset. The subject of the sunset is noise.

My method of describing the sunset, its noise, is likewise noise: Instagram, Facebook, Twitter, Tumblr. Already I know that I will inevitably sully the sun's purity of empty pitch with references to violence, death, hierarchy, money.

If silence can be sullied.

(Can it?)

1.2

Jacques Attali writes of Brueghel's painting *Carnival's Quarrel with Lent:* "his angst is audible." In Brueghel's paintings, the clatter of human noise prefigures *silence as power*, specifically, the silencing of social order, of religious morality. The church's policing of festival and carnival, of pagan joy, willed silence on the people and on their landscape. This was long before industry replaced festival and carnival as noise, before the air roared with turbines and silence split into two different ends: silence as luxury, silence as torture.

Silence as luxury: John Cage in Harvard's anechoic chamber.

Silence as torture: Unknown unknown in solitary. Guantanamo Bay. Water drip. Electricity down the back. Ray Bradbury's Margot in *All Summer in a Day*, the girl whose peers lock her away for knowing the sun, "how like a lemon it was, and how hot." Her punishment: a closet. On the only day in seven years when the Venusian inhabitants would witness the rising and falling of their lifeblood.

At the end of the story: "They walked over to the closet door slowly and stood by it. Behind the closet door was only silence. They unlocked the door, even more slowly, and let Margot out."

1.3

I like to imagine that when Margot steps out of the closet, *Carrie* begins to play.

Silence is bad movie candy dissolving on my tongue, and then it's in me, heavy, like a velvet blacklight painting of a sunset.

SWF ISO someone to test my food for poison. SWF ISO a different formula for luminescent blood.

2.1

A memory, a scrap: Mary Ruefle quoting Cy Twombly quoting John Crowe Ransom's scrap of paper: "The image cannot be dispossessed of a primordial freshness which ideas can never claim."

The sound of an image of a sunset is noise; John Cage taught us that noise is music.

The sound of a fresh idea about an image of the sunset is words; Ferdinand de Saussure taught us that words are ransom.

(Correction: it's I who use the word *ransom*. I told you I wouldn't be able to discuss the sunset without sullying it with violence and death.)

2.2

(Words are money; words are music:

Can you imagine the value, volume of

the collected ransom letters for

what has been silenced?)

2.3

Ransom's *primordial freshness.*

"This stuff is really fresh!"

Fab 5 Freddy's primordial "fresh!" is one of the most duplicated motifs in music history. Sampled over 900 times, "fresh!" makes its first appearance as repetition in Herbie Hancock's "Rockit," the first hit song to feature pure noise: the scratch. The scratch (noise) compelled to percussion (noise punctured—systematized—ordered—by silence) stutters into the future: *"F-F-F-F-Fresh!"*

(The sunset is also a scratch, skipping: the sun sets, the sun sets, the sun sets...)

2.4

Note: I said, "the first hit song" not "the first song."

There is no way to ascertain precisely which song was the first song to feature pure noise.

(Was it a rock against a tree branch?)

Origins are elusive.

We can only hope to understand the first *recorded* dissonance, if we can locate the document.

(Now it's easier:

#nofilter #BrooklynBridge #sunset)

3

Once, on a road trip x-country, I drove through Truth or Consequences, NM, listening to Radiohead's *Exit Music*. I thought of my friend J in Oakland, how he always wanted to start a band called *Exit Music*, and then there was a song called *Exit Music*, and then a day after that there was a band called *Exit Music*, because no idea originates at a single point of origin.

Charles Darwin wasn't the only man to think up evolution. Alfred Russel Wallace, a young unknown naturalist, wrote a letter to Darwin describing a theory of evolution (though he didn't call it Evolution) by natural selection (not by that Name, either) well before Darwin published *On the Origin of Species*.

The roots of ideas are quantum-entangled.

Attributes are assigned not to firsts, but to the namers of things.

An image of a sunset on a postcard; on its opposing side, my handwriting: *Dear J, I drove through Truth or Consequences. I didn't stop for gas.*

4.1

A terror, a scrap: Fernando Pessoa writes: "I fell, with every sunset, against my hopes and certainties."

I fall, with every sunset, against my origins, against the complexity of my identity. Which will not survive the substance of that which I create.

Says Deleuze. (And just about everyone else.) And Ben Lerner adds, "given men as they are: asthmatic, out of tune and time."

4.2

I close my book. The sun alights on the California coastline. The man I mistakenly love turns to me and says: "No matter the key, you sing out of it."

I've been humming along to a neighboring vehicle's radio. I swipe and tap my phone and frame the horizon with the camera's viewfinder.

That's when he says: "The world doesn't need any more photographs of sunsets."

4.3

My response: "I disagree."

My response: Ancient cultures worshipped the sun; the sound of ritual worship is music. (The sound of the sun is silence.) Late capitalism's inhabitants can't take enough awesome pix of sunsets; the sound of ritual representation is noise. (The sound of the sun is still silence.) (I upload my sunset

selfie to Instagram; I can't keep myself from the ritual, the narrative; I'm human; the world aims and shoots through me, like sound, like radiation, and I receive and release it, the signal, my image of self, my sunset representation; its noise belongs to the world; as the sun cradles its radioactive isotopes before they pulse into waves, disperse into particles, before they're extinguished into matter, before the sun sets, before the sunlight is repurposed as heat, moon, flashlight . . .)

5.1

Memory: Mid-summer. Everyone I know can't sleep. One friend says it's biological. The long day. Another friend says it's the vibrations of the celestial spheres. I say it's the vibration of concrete, air traffic and wi-fi, the hum of conditioning. Behavioral conditioning. Air conditioning. Aimless walking. Animal pacing.

I walk to the park, sit on a bench, and listen to the thrum of the FDR ricochet from glass to glass. Thinking, there must be a word for the drone that underscores the city. There must be a word for the hand that's acutely aware of the need to hold something other than the surface of concrete, house keys, blue jean pockets.

I can't escape the heat. I can never get away from myself. My hair needs combing. My hair needs conditioning, too. Me, my self, my hair—we're in it for the long haul.

I click play and an advertisement stutters:

CASINO OF THE EARTH. CASINO OF THE SKY. CASINO OF THE WIND.

5.2

We're living in a golden era of listicles, you and I. Listicles of obsolete pigments: Maya blue, Tyrian purple, White Lead, Lapis Lazuli, Mummy brown, ultramarine and Dragon's Blood red. Lyrics from the internet: *Trust no one. Women have chainsaws inside. Men have daisies and softness.* The harmless pests: Book lice, silverfish, springtails. Spiders that look like raspberries the size of pinheads. Emerging artists with made-up names: Carbon, Bell. Advice for pissing on another's piss scent. 21 ways to learn to say "I'm busy" so it sounds like an axe. How to glue your work to your lapel.

And now we're moving farther and farther from the matter at hand.

And now we're moving farther and farther away from matter.

5.3

It's true, capitalism has learned to survive with art as a chronic condition.

Parasite, virus, cancer—which sickness?

Art needs a specialist.

Art needs to multiply like RNA and compound interest. The tyranny of art's infection is that art is indistinguishable from both money and its host.

5·4

Like a film, the artist "doesn't give you what you desire, [he] tells you how to desire." (Slavoj Žižek's speaking of cinema; cinema is a subset of art.)

The role of the artist is not to make art, but to show others how to be an artist. To make *being an artist* desirable. How to transmogrify one's self and one's desires into cultural currency. How to inculcate one's currency in the tissues of a brain. How to calcify the neural pathways.

If we cannot discern the cause of the patient's distress, we cannot cure the patient. If we cannot determine what is art and what is not art, we cannot excise art from capital. We cannot exterminate the vector. We cannot extricate the tumor. We can only mitigate the pain. Nerves fire about the site of attachment. Art migrates to the brain.

This is the tepid joy of symbiosis. When everything is art, the artist inhabits a world of hospital confetti. The world is safe and colorful and morbid like a terminally ill toddler's birthday. Everything is tragicomedy under the veneer of capital Art.

Michelangelo says, "I remove everything that doesn't look like David" and we pull away the BPA-laced sippy cup and the tumor blooms fluorescent in the baby.

When I remove everything that doesn't look like David, I fall asleep.

5.5

I read the listicles, not for content or amusement, but for their transparency:

Top X artists of XXXX
X Under X Emerging Artists
Top X Emerging Artists To Watch

We don't watch the art, we watch the artist. We watch the artist *emerge*. We desire *emergence*. The artist teaches us to desire *emergence*. Walter Benjamin teaches us to classify conditions of *emergence*.

"The trembling child emerges from behind the curtain," writes Sarah Manguso. *"Unchain my heart, thou monstrous god."*

    (Unchain from what?)

    (Star dust?)

5.6

The artist shows us how to desire a star at a threshold: Nebulae cloud the supernova; the star composes, about to collapse. The art star shows us how and why and what to use when we, like stars, consume our own gas. We no longer *amuse ourselves to death*. We aren't amused. This is a terminally ill toddler's birthday party. We'll celebrate ourselves, like Whitman. We'll celebrate ourselves to death.

Watch the baby scream.
Watch the baby sprout
a poet who sprouts a love

poem abounding
in metaphors of war.
Watch the war

sprout a middle manager
sprout the baby poet write

There must be a word for
        the art of willful self-deceit
There must be a word for
        the establishment of a holistic body
There must be a word for
        performing a whole
There must be a word for
        branded optimism
There must be a word for
        discreet luxury
There must be a word for
        a fascination with a faltering myth
There must be a word for
        a utopia that never arrives
There must be a word for
        how goals are scaled by the typical
There must be a word for

                        unstable connection due to
                        variance in bandwidth

There must be a word for how, in negative criticism, the critic takes up more space than the artist, like an overweight individual on an economy flight

There must be a word for how, in negative criticism, the critic displays his faculties like a statuette of a knife

5.8

I didn't set out to write about art or noise or human behavior. I set out only to gawk at the supermoon. My mind match-cuts to a different moon:

> *Who do you think you are? Derrida?* the established poet asks. Under the echo's weaker example. He means to shame me into performing my gender. I could slap him, but I don't. Not because I respect him, but because capital has conditioned me to respect the space between objects.

> My mind match-cuts to a different but similar scene:

I sit on a bench and listen to the thrum of the FDR ricochet in the spaces between objects. I listen to girls and young men complain about the dimensions of their apartments. I listen to a dog bark. It barks. I listen to the movement of the air.

6.1

I could try feedback analysis. I could manage my identity like a hedge fund. I could speculate on the risk of taking up too much space, of taking too much time. I could write a meditation on age, on legacy, on red. A meditation on the ocean. I could consider what circumstances dictate the access one has to a sunset or an ocean or the body of a woman. I could consider celebrity and age. How age is rebranded to resemble tradition using an image of an aging celebrity on a beach. I could give a sunset's consideration to beauty and duration and rarity. But a sunset is never enough.

The oldest gesture in the history of history is the sound that escapes a man as he's looking outwards over a horizon. ("Farewell, Farewell / Beheaded sun," speaks the close of Apollinaire's "Zone." Oliver Bernard, translation.)

I, too, am looking outwards over a horizon, translating a zone into language. Times Square, the view from the 33rd floor: a horizon lost to a montage of horizons. The evaporation encoded within an economy as webbed as our system of unnamed stars. Entangled, collectors draw the haunted hallways of their neural pathways through the exhibit at the Zabludowicz Collection. Which is also a horizon: commerce at its limit.

A gallery is a horizon: the place at which the art and viewer appear to meet.

Collectors, artists, collectors of artists. Pearl earrings. Real perfume. Scent lingers, so much that I wonder if the room will ever empty. The kind of scent that leads you to say, *that's real perfume.* (I don't mind using *you, you* the personal, *you* the universal, *you* the now, *you* the ever, to address or evoke simultaneously presence and absence. I'm inclusive of the unspecific, not inconsistent.)

Present or absent, when we leave, the perfume, the floor will be.

6.2

Jean-Jacques Rousseau says that the distinctive quality of a sentient being, no, an "active or intelligent being," is the being's ability "to give a sense to the word *is*." (*Sentient* can perceive but might not know it perceives.)

> And yet, the floor *is*.
> And the view *is*.
> And the montage *is*.

> It's that luminescent.

And I arrive as I am: dressed in layers, a late-aughts period costume. I'm late. I was *taking too much time*. I've anticipated my entrance like the presence of a security camera. My eyes on the room like a hand on a thigh.

How are you supposed to clean it up, someone says. *How are you supposed to listen. Look at me,* someone says, *I—Because it's baggage, more baggage now than when I left and this time I left because there isn't enough money.*

There is more than enough money, etc.

This is not the room where we don't watch TV while we don't eat Chinese as a dog barking is silenced in the background. No one in the room is doused with acne as potent as gasoline. No one's talking about gasoline. Perhaps they speak of oil. Too young to leave, too old not to imagine already having left.

6.3

I think of Yves Klein commenting on the "public prisoners" at the private view where he first revealed his monochrome surfaces.

Klein's viewers saw, not paintings, but a decorative display.

They perceived decoration. Mosaic. Hospital confetti: a fiesta of color arranged to delight, to amuse, but most importantly, to distract from what truly captivated: the other patrons. The magnetic attractions and repulsions between human bodies. Klein's paintings were demoted to wallpaper. What fascinated Klein was how the gathering of people before product, the ambient drone of subjects congregated before objects, the zone of the product's, no— the painting's, no— the *color's*, event, was the art.

It comes as no surprise that in Klein's later performance piece, *Zone de Sensibilité Picturale Immatérielle (Zones of Immaterial Pictorial Sensibility)*, he offered empty spaces in exchange for gold.

6.4

Hospital confetti scatters here, too, in the ornamental sound.

Sound is the main course, not the garnish. The fanfare, not the flourish. Leslie Flanagan's speaker cabinets churn with repetitions; the volume is sufficient to claim a stake in the landscape. I listen with intent, but instead of hearing palpitations, I hear the crowd. I hear ironed hair, pressed black silk, kidskin wallets. Italian combat boots with gap tooth soles. Complimentary bags of Sun Chips. Windowpanes and HVAC. And like Attali listening to Brueghel, I hear each source, isolated and in unison. And the view, its 33 stories. The view is the loudest voice in the gallery.

"Monet's first water lily . . . repeats all the others," writes Deleuze, invoking Charles Péguy. And on the gallery's lower level, the lilies', confetti's arpeggios: Peter Fischli and David Weiss's terriers bark and bark and bark under the rudder of rumor, the stiletto clatter, the whir of Cory Arcangel's gyrating purple cubes. I hear Arcangel's autotuned Hendrix, Seth Price's pitch-shifted Ronald Reagan assassination attempt, repeat. Expensive attempts to fix the past.

And like Attali listening to Brueghel, I join the crowd. I read the lower-level view, its 7 stories.

Even on the lower level, the view is the loudest voice in the gallery.

> If the art can't awe the crowd into silence
> If the art can't silence the crowd

18

If the only thing that will silence the crowd
is the gallery

when the gallery closes

6.5

Though its origins are unknown, the quote: "History is written by the victors" is often attributed to Winston Churchill.

(Origins of attributes
are quantum-entangled.)

(History progresses from noise to noise,
punctuated by silences.)

A internet search on my phone informs me that the first recorded "OMG" has also been attributed to Winston Churchill.

(Origins of slang are quantum-entangled.)

(History is percussive.)

Baudelaire writes: "When the cruel sun strikes with increased blows / The city, the country, the roofs, and the wheat fields, / I go alone to try my fanciful fencing, / Scenting in every corner the chance of a rhyme." (William Aggeler, translation.)

Hancock's album is entitled
Future Shock (1983), preceded by

James Brown's television series,
Future Shock (1976–1978), preceded by

Curtis Mayfield's minor hit,
"Future Shock" (1973), preceded by

Future Shock, a (1972) documentary
based on Alvin Toffler's book,

Future Shock (1970).
"A cock is a dick" —Ariana Reines

With whom do you sympathize: silence or noise?

6.6

Deleuze reminds us that the history of thought should be approached as though
it were collage. Ideas, new and old, remain concurrently present in a future idea's
formation.

I take this to mean: take what you like and run with it.

Any source can be expressive.

6.7

Curated noise takes expensive Modernism one step further: First, it clears the room of the ordinary, then it clears the room of ordinary people. ("This is the sound of that anything becoming a cool thing.")

If you clear the room, does that make you an influence? ("This is the sound of that cool thing becoming a warm thing.")

Do you know that your benefactor is an arms dealer? ("This is the sound of that warm thing gaining speed.")

What does the space between your body and your patron's body, your benefactor's body, your curator's body, a massacred body, mean to you? ("This is the sound of that speed gathering history.")

Does it make you mean? ("This is the sound of that history being transformed into an item.")

Does it make you feel like you're packing heat? ("This is the sound of that item being duplicated.")

Whose war have you been coerced to speak? ("This is the sound of that duplicate being used.")

Who's satisfied with merely existing? ("This is the sound of that using being performed by a machine.")

If war is a work of limited duration. ("This is the sound of that machine producing a material.")

If space is a work of limited duration. ("This is the sound of that material becoming liquid.")

If a gallery is a work of limited duration. If an audience is a work of limited duration. If a critic is a work of limited duration. If you are a work of limited duration. If you and your lover and the collection and the public and the curator and the art and the war ("This is the sound of that liquid becoming an object.")

Does your art demand incorporation into the masters? ("This is the sound of that object becoming a service.")

Does your art's brand scar the viewer long after its placard has been replaced? ("This is the sound of that service being outsourced.")

Who dictates your curatorial statement? ("This is the sound of that outsourcing being cast in concrete.")

Sound wishes to be free. ("This is the sound of that cast concrete being thrown from the 33rd floor.") ("This is the sound of that floor being streamlined.") ("This is the sound of that streamlining being pictured.")

Sound—like white phosphorous—cannot be packaged without a leak. ("This is the sound of that picture turning to clay.")

The leak is a featured design element. ("This is the sound of that clay being colored.")

People die from leaks. ("This is the sound of that color communicating.") ("This is the sound of that communication being internalized.") ("This is the sound") ("This is the sound") ("This is the sound of that internalizing being transformed into sound.")

Don't police my tone. I'm conscious of my cadence.

6.8

I'm an artist. I cop an attitude to give my voice the characteristic of singularity.

Macklemore's "Thrift Shop"; Justin Bieber's "Right Here"; Linkin Park's "Cure for the Itch"; "On and On" by Missy Elliot; The Beastie Boys' "Sure Shot" and "Intergalactic"; "Boyz-N-The-Hood" by Eazy-E; "Pump Up the Volume" by MARRS; "The Look" by Roxette; "Girl You Know It's True" by Milli Vanilli; "So Fresh" by Will Smith; "Sin" by Nine Inch Nails.

You can make a list, depriving the list's constituent items of their active ingredient: time.

You can delight in the list's formal elements: variation, substitution, elaboration.

You can ring history's chimes: Art is doorbell. Art lets you know when History has arrived. A group show is a Home Depot aisle of doorbells. Ply the angular appliqué and dead ends will spin in the reel.

("And this is the sound of that sound.")

A body exists only with and through its cry.

(A night of silence is luxury.)

(A silenced night is torture.)

6.9

The old night is a vibration in the new night's surface. And vice versa: The new day is a vibration in the old day's surface. The old new day had Benjamin's arcades, it had clear glass, then blue glass and green glass and yellow glass and buildings like lemon slices spritzed the sky. The new new day is black slickness, the spectrum reflected in oily obliqueness.

Literally: The Times Square skyscraper windows are black mirrors. The sun's glare, the stock market ticker, beat on black glass and black granite and multicolored foam. Reflections barrel backwards towards their sources. Like letters marked "Return to Sender." ("Return to Sender," written by Winfield Scott and Otis Blackwell, recorded by Elvis, echoes in the stairwell. Elvis, who's left no forwarding address: "I gave a letter to the postman,

> he put it his sack.
> Bright in early next morning,
> he brought my letter back.")

J tweets: "Perhaps the only difference between me and other people is that I've always demanded more from the sunset."

If the difference
between black glass and blue-green glass is
        an essential design element

        If the differences
between repetition, reverberation, echo, feedback, pure tones, wave sums,
harmonics, and ambient frequencies are
        essential design elements

        If the sum
of repetition, reverberation, echo, feedback, pure tones, wave sums, harmonics,
and ambient frequencies
        each with their own political character are
        the quality of drone

        If the quality
of silence is the sum
of a system's damping power

        If the quality
of silence is the absence
of oscillation as event

        If nothing can silence
the artwork but the museum
when the museum closes

If there are artists who fail to participate
in the erecting of museums
      If there are artists who refuse to participate
in the erecting of museums
      If there are artists who participate
in the erecting of museums
but sweeten the plaster

      "we need museums" —Greek chorus

      If an artist's aspiration to singularity
      If an artwork's aspiration to singularity

takes shape only in the artist's relationships
      with other artists
takes shape only in the artwork's relationship
      to other artworks

      If the meaning of an artwork
(if meaning exists)
      lies in its difference from other artworks
(if other exists)
      the curator got this right:

an artwork will not stand alone.

      (Make a fist, squeeze it, that's your heart.
      Let the voice in your head be the loudest.

You, love, are a frequency
on a Roman road.)

7.1

Times Square, through glass: American silence. Each eye, each lens, closes, opens
on one point, on one day, at one moment. Close in. Like hunting. Where the ball.
Like Fat Man. With its 33,000 panels. Where spiral. Like thermonuclear science.
Like a white van sniper. Like an active shooter simulation. Like the Navy Yard.
Like Newtown on television. Where I grew up. Men, marks, the marks of days.
Where everyone knows where and how they're standing. Where "I can erect no
safety rail," I echo Mike Kelley echoing Balzac. "I want to sing murder," I echo
Mike Kelley echoing Balzac. "I want to sing murder." Under the Janus-faced sun.
Roman numerals go the way of Roman roads. *What happened on that day.*

"Return to sender, address unknown
No such number, no such zone."

Light data, atmospheric particles, an unimpeded hue: a blue monochrome.

"My pursuit of the indefinable," Yves Klein says.

"I hear the wings of the crows beating cymbals loudly above a world whose flood
Van Gogh can apparently no longer contain," says Antonin Artaud.

"The water is blue,
not a water-blue,

27

but a liquid paint blue.
The suicided madman has been there
and given the water of paint back to nature,
but who will give it back to him?"

"It is the painter that becomes blue," says Deleuze.

And now, along the avatars of our reducible selves, our infinitely divisible pursuits. Our infinitely divisible terror. Our fracked colors.

I once wrote a poem:

I deboned myself.
My favorite colors of frosting
were red, yellow, orange.

7.2

What we're safe from. What we're free from. What negative liberty we've given the cloud. What we've lost to the language of loss.

Cost language. Garbage language. Gyre language. Language of husk and wrapper. Glyphs crowning. Rise above the babble and into historical lisp like a pencil tip dragged along the jet-ragged corridors. Across Sony surfaces, Steinway surfaces. Through plumes where pipes hoist water into negative space. Into checkerboards where every square is black and the pawns are absent. Every vector accounted for until the fear unfolds domestically like a napkin under the table.

And I am. Emotionally turned out like a reversible raincoat. I have been employed by many corporations. I have been employed by the sound I make with my hands. I am alloy, American. I know the sky's been hung. My past is flammable, paper and plastic. My heart is flammable, too. It burns because it is the heir of centuries.

The centuries burn beyond the paywall. The paywall burns because it is the heir of fists.

Hunger Games billboards stripe the marquees: Young people are drawn to the performance of theatrical militancy.

It's best to be sublime, like pain. To pain we are subservient.

7.3

Disney characters. The strawberry glass. The lemon basil smash-cut LCD. The lavender splash. The orange zest dizzy. With strawberry girls swimming with dolphins. On the licorice NASDAQ. Of the apple's red ring. The classical sorbet. A Roman rose ringed with Roman numerals. A grid of expiry. Flashing at increasingly faster frame rates. Than those to which I've been accustomed. Biological eye: Here there is a God: Here, we participate. With breath and violet candy. DIY God. Debutante God. Diversified, divested, denuded.

I have an occult book I found on a ledge with me in my pocket. *The Brotherhood of Light—Divination** advises: "Repetition is divination." Its advice: *Pay attention to the sunrise.* There is a notion of the clue-ness of things, like codecs in poems. Horizons in creases. A real girl, a strawberry. A shadow economy of contraband women. And all we fight for in the developing world.

*In the future, poetry
will colonize
genre

In the future,
poetry will poach
the sun

The past
will no longer
sundown

Our poetry
Our colony
of futures

Our genre
of future

Our
virtuoso

labor of
        Poem
        Sun
        Imperialist
        Adventure
        Polemic against
        Cycles

Radical
Without nuance
Henchman
God-
Burned
Song

7.4

Gerri Granger's reply to "Return to Sender"—"(Return to Sender) Don't Want
Your Letters"— was also released under the title "Don't Want Your Love Letters."

Why two titles? Released in 1962 as two 45 RPM singles on Bigtop Records, the
writing credits are attributed to Otis Blackwell, Winfield Scott, and Ben Raleigh.
Raleigh penned the lyrics. Granger sings:

> "They say I got a love letter.
> The writing didn't change."

I want Gerri to sing: "The writing hadn't changed."

I want an acknowledgement of the habitual letter-writer's many different canceled
stamps, letters rewritten and sealed and sent, received, returned unopened. But
there it is: "The writing *didn't change*." No matter how many times Granger looked
at the envelope, the writing *didn't change*. Same stamp, same cancellation, same
name, same address in the same script. Endlessly returned to her: in her mailbox,
the envelope, again, again, as though *the exact same letter arrived each time*.

There: the singularity, the hit, its repeated arrival. Despite any promise, any pretense of revolution, of pleasure provided *if only,* the truth of the modulation occurs only after the repeated pop hook: Change happens where it is forbidden.

And then there is the background static that crackles beneath the music.

7.5

Some nights
I turn on
my laptop, click on

William Basinski's *Disintegration Loops*

His video of the sunset
His liner notes:

"the music was dying"

7.6

Some nights
I feel very close to Walter Benjamin, I can almost feel his body (no, that's not an unearthed grave, that's my bedroom, those are my unwashed sheets.)

Some nights
I wish Walter Benjamin had lived to load a page, lay in bed, take a selfie.

I wish he'd lived long enough to upload his selfie to Facebook, Instagram, Tumblr, Twitter, after the sun's gone down. I wonder what Walter Benjamin would've thought about the infinite replication of one's worst character flaws. I wonder what he would've thought about a flaw's use value.

I wish Walter Benjamin had lived to peel off yoga pants. To join a throng of women and men in identical pants, holding identical poses, intoning the repeated "Om."

I wish Walter Benjamin had lived to learn about hedge fund managers and stochastic processes. I wish he had lived to learn how financial analysts and data journalists study Zen meditation as a means of decentering themselves from the narrative. I mean, their narrative.

In our culture of confession, one of our greatest crimes still seems to be that of positing oneself at the center of a narrative.

Some nights
If Walter Benjamin were alive, he'd be more than a celebrity. He'd be famous. If not for his cultural commentary, then surely for being The World's Oldest Man. Pure singularity. What would be the condition of emergence he'd zone in on: School shootings? Black glass?

7.7

Some nights
I feel very close to black glass

I feel very close to its buildings' blueprints
because blueprints are collectively drafted

Some nights
I feel very close

to the brute politics of men
Some nights

If I have not yet left the gallery, I fear
I never will

(Not true:
Though in the gallery,

I experience emotions;
I fear nothing in the gallery)

Some nights
I fear nothing, not even my failure

in changing, or saving, the gallery, knowing
only part of the gallery
can be saved or changed

(Some nights
J tweets: "Imagine saying, 'That sunset is interesting.' —Susan Sontag")

I feel the sun
about to set, the sky
about to glaze

7.8

Some nights
I think of Marina Abramović, her first painting lesson:

"He threw turpentine and gasoline onto the canvas, put a lit match in the middle, and everything exploded. Then he looked at me and said, 'This is a sunset,' and left."

Her teacher, Yves Klein.

7.9

Some nights
I watch individual members of the crowd lean into the installation, attentively or distractedly, into each color, each sound, each shape, as someone in the group asks a question, as someone on the fringe or at the center offers a word that shuttles the discussion forward

Some nights
the crowd becomes more a constellation, less a dispersion through its participation; some take notes for pieces and projects and texts and lectures and performances at which they will reconvene, repeating themselves, repeating each other, exchanging suggestions and retractions

(camellia, rose, and oud,
dirt carpet, ragged grout)

(there exists no room
in which we don't leave

a trace, a suggestion)

An institution will love one or two individuals, and one or two will carry the others, in text, in memory, in reference, in script

And each and every one will want and need and desire more, becoming more and more themselves in each and every day's dawning, middle, and close

And in their tedious and soothing everyday practices, their tics, their to-buy and to-do lists, beckons the horizon whose actual hue not even the most precise meteorological or quantum investment algorithm could one day predict, and in this color an eventual darkness, and in this darkness another darkness, another horizon, another flawed algorithm, another event, another cause and effect, another prediction's neglect, another darkness in the darkness

And the color of the sun is not yellow

And the color of snow is not white

As Yves Klein's purity of concept, of blue, exists in palette, but in the corporeal realm, the realm of performance, of actualization, is contaminated by context

Or should I say, transformed, as black skyscraper mirrors wane blue, then yellow, rouge, each color pure in its duration, only to be bronzed and delivered to darkness as dusk delivers darkness

And in the darkness, sunrise

And in the sunrise, sunset

SNOW

THE BEGINNING IS SIMPLE: THE MOON RISES

The road winds. Snow falls on many, many trees. Inside the house, the family keeps warm with electric heat. The television shows are broadcast over and over. The paintings are painted over and over. And I have nothing left to say other than: I don't want to repeat anything.

I am a tune the universe will whistle before whistling the tune of someone else. You are a tune I will whistle for a while. I don't want to sing anyone else.

I don't know how to snow over a city, how to freeze a world with a gesture. The kind of gesture they talk about when they speak of Marilyn or Baldwin, way back in the 20th century. I no longer live or look anywhere consistently. This should be freeing. I should feel free. I live in a country where people who love each other keep each other warm with space heaters and romantic commodities.

The important part of the snowstorm isn't the outcome. There are no outcomes. André Breton taught me this. No, Breton taught me there are no causes. He taught me there is no logical progression from love to Linux.

I clearly remember reading a lie about John Lennon: that he fell in love with Yoko Ono when he climbed a ladder to read her tiny script on the ceiling of a gallery: *yes*. That's when he knew, they say. It isn't true. Chronologically, he'd fallen for her already. But the myth, the water, it's thirsty for a listener.

On Twitter, the fake Nietzsche tweets: "I tried to lift the ocean and fell in love with the sea." I cut and paste the sentiment: "I tried to lift the ocean and fell in love with the sea. I tried to lift the ocean and fell in love with the sea. I tried to lift the ocean" then retweet another user: "Eventually your heart is a bartender who cuts you off."

The most important part of snow isn't the water, isn't the outcome. There is no snow other than flux. Night comes, and in the headlights, parabolas. Bands of ice in the clay pot. The patterns impressed in space are the patterns we'll fix in memory, our little affirmations. They tell us, *yes*, it snowed. They tell us, *yes,* us.

SMALL TRUE THINGS

1. OUTLIERS BEDAZZLE THE NEWS

J train body density has increased since winter began. I'm as patient as I can be in the morning, patient with my terrible similes like *bodies split the cars like overcooked sausages* in the push and shove as the doors open and close. Backpacks and black plastic sacks; garlic sweat, carbon monoxide, and pleather. A hand slips down the pole; someone says, "sorry." The tallest men swipe the ceiling for stability. I think: *Isn't that the way.*

Beside me, a girl melts to the floor. *Ladies and gentlemen, we are paused momentarily.* She cradles her head with her mittens. A man offers his seat. She shakes her head. *Due to train traffic ahead.*

The car jerks forward. The buildings tick past, the turquoise townhouse, the checkerboard midcentury, the high rise with five bikes on four balconies. What my eye rests on foretells my mood for the rest of the ride, which is the whole ride, my mood rising like steam from the tracks. The gaze has always been an omen scratched in the world.

The piece of me that surrenders to others finds a home here.

When the train isn't crowded, I read *The New York Times,* the epic scrolling up my week like film credits. The epic has everything to do with the accrual of bits and series and wholes and the missing figure of the poet, who was replaced by the critic, who was replaced by the data analyst, squinting into a grainy cellphone image of a room she'd recently left. I wonder if I'll ever appear in *The New York Times.* I wonder who I'll haunt. Everything epic is personal. I cross, uncross my legs. The epic is where my form surrenders.

At the last stop, I exit the train, leave the station. It's raining. The cobblestones remind me of how phenomena surface with no explanation. How there is no one effort I could expend to induce or prevent what happens when I look a man in the eye as we pass each other in front of the Stock Exchange. I have the overwhelming desire to be sweet to him. I have the overwhelming desire to write *I love him, I love him*. But mostly, I have the overwhelming desire to be equal.

2. STUDDED WITH MEMORIES LIKE MICA-STREWN SHALE

Country and city are created in tandem. What is extracted from dirt rises in air. Granite and sandstone and marble glow with the heat of noon, heat reflected not from the ripple of a river, but from the crosshatched ribbons of asphalt and tar. Onion bulbs are sliced and served on porcelain a hundred miles from their roots; the cotton wicks of candles ignite on copper tables. The soul of a collection of field-sung words becomes a tune, becomes pop music, a historical force.

I drive from city to country and back again, maps in my glove box, maps in my car door pockets, maps in a plastic bucket in the trunk. Hand-drawn maps in blue ballpoint pen with shaggy spiral notebook manes, maps without addresses, without proper names. These maps are exercises in dream interpretation: *Where was I going? What forces directed me?* Like dreams, their symbols threaten to dissolve when exposed to the sun. Their stories seem more awake than the continually refreshing GPS. Alert to historical depths, they remember where the roads and power lines didn't used to be.

(Does the gnarled grammar I use to express this reveal an unconscious desire to obliterate? Ever since the Babylonians carved a moon into clay, words have been at war to reclaim their worldless state.)

On the highway, memory glimmers surface: the smell of dead leaves before I had a word for it (petrichor); the sense of pain and unease in my gut before I had a word for it (stomachache); how late one autumn, a professor taught me that the word *stomachache* sets humans apart from animals. *Dogs can't express what's wrong,* he said. *All they can do is circle; all they know is what is; they don't understand difference; they don't understand stomach or intestine; they don't understand that others have stomachs, others have intestines.*

What I took from the conversation was this: that the word *stomachache* contains the entirety of human history.

At a red light, I watch my one dog intuitively know the ailments of the other. How sensitive she is to the other's ear pain, gut nausea, malaise in the summer heat when the water bowl is low and lacking ice; how they acknowledge each other's sensitivities with a phantom but equally existent language. Their modest wish is to be acknowledged. How similar we are.

3 . IN THE PROBABLE SHAPES OF A CONCRETE UNIVERSE

Granite steps lead to the ruins of an era when a mountain was an industrial resource. Now its open space is marker of leisure and when I cruise up the road that winnows to a path to its vista, I feel the nascent edge of story roughing up inside me, against the brilliant visual, against the deciduous palette. How self-centered it is to consider anything a resource.

I know things are going well when I don't need to consider the past, too enraptured by the forward-pulsing process I feel when I find myself, one foot ahead of the other, on the trail, as though the print I leave, its traces of rubber and polyamide and carbon dioxide, doesn't exist. How self-centered it is to believe in the eternal *now*; how self-centered it is to *keep moving*.

The quarry is deep with water, the mine system flooded with water. I can hear the wet echo when I lean into the tunnels' locked gates. The mountain is honeycombed with flood like a hive flush with honey. It smells of lichen and snowmelt. As though the world is saying: *Where there is a crime, time will dissolve it.*

The mica I pull from the rubble is embedded with light the way I remain studded with dreams long after I wake. Mica is derived from the Latin *mica*, meaning *a crumb,* and, *micare to glitter.* There is no pristine wilderness but there are filaments of stars in all detritus, the heat of the sun in what exits the daylight. There is no pristine forgiveness, but there is a glut of kindness in this image I excavate for you.

At the base of mountain are the remains of a mining town, Charybes, named after the mythic monster, Charybdis. In Aristotle's *Meteorologica*, Charybdis takes one swallow of the ocean and the mountain tops rise into view. After a second gulp, entire islands surface. Her third drink will dry the oceans forever. *Thirsty woman*. I'd like to consider geological time without collapsing into myth, but I can only touch the granite shelf as I pass it.

Granite reminds me that the farthest my human imagination can reach is the limit of cultural time. I can't endeavor to create anything that will equal or outlast the mountain, not even a progeny or a space program. My modest wish is to be remembered. It is the wish of all of us.

4. IN THE JEWELBOX OF CHILDHOOD

I once believed that lily pads floated free like saucer islands, atomized on the water's surface. It wasn't until my toes clenched the edge of the sun-bleached dock, when I dove and breast-stroked into the harp of cords that strung the pads to the bottom, that I realized that they, too, are anchored.

The dank lake alcove is shellacked with lily pads. My legs tangle the underwater stems, submerging the pads where I swim, the water, lukewarm tea. Cave water warmed by the sun, the slick velvet algae verdant between my toes. The odor of honey and sulfur linger where a blossom offers an oasis to a yellow jacket, a red ant on a petal's lip—how did he arrive here, so far from shore?

A dragonfly more like a barbed jewel than like itself. A static of mosquitos when the humidity rises like pressure applied by a damp washcloth.

At the far end of the alcove, an outlet leaks into the black lake, supermassive and ice cold, rocked by waves from distant speedboats that threaten to capsize the aluminum row boat I captain by myself. I'm afraid to cross the vast black lake so instead I skirt the shore, navigating the neighboring nooks, the ridges of roots that escalate into timber, the lichen-crowned stones. In the amber shallows, sandy nests of sunnies nip my toes when I dip my feet too close to their homes.

Black flies and horseflies angle for the kill; bluebottles drone when death is already in the proximity. And the water sliders, water skaters, june bugs, and moths.

How can you be sure that oblivion doesn't love you?

A hawk soars for what seems like hours, idly, then pins his wings to his body and dives. He cracks the surface of the black lake and the lake recoils. The spray dissolves into a rainbow. The hawk rises to half-mast, half his original altitude. A white belly buoys in the ripples. The raptor dives again, sears the fish with his talons, wings pumping. I could touch him with an oar. Then he takes off—straight across the lake towards the opposite shore, as people do in the city, people who idle on curbsides scrolling through newsfeeds, refreshing their screens, then suddenly, irrevocably, cut through the street.

5. A BLACK GEL PILL I CAN TAKE INDEFINITELY

My mother pirouettes on her skate's rubber stopper and glides backwards onto the floor. I clomp after her in my rentals. The dancers, who dazzle the crowd in sequin leotards under the disco ball, grab my mother's hands and twirl her. With no amount of practice can I attain the grace she embodies. I grip the bannister and watch from the wall. Even as a young girl, my temperament is best suited not to the execution, but to the observation of kinetic beauty.

When the temperature drops, the fire department floods the town hall parking lot with lake water. It freezes overnight into a black tray of ice. A lone lamp on a telephone pole offers a meager spotlight.

Night on the makeshift ice rink: a capsule memory, a narcotic suspended in the soluble rim of my body. The moonless sky, the electric wires that ring the lamp, the parabolas of distant headlights, they harden, become more certain in memory. Beyond the curb, the chain link fence's white quilt ascends from the irascible overgrowth; remnants of a snow squall crumble like sugar cubes onto the asphalt; and my mother skates loops in the center of all of it; my mother skates late into the night; my mother skates the shape of a question mark just beyond the halo of light.

In *La Jetée*, Chris Marker suggests that the images from our childhood that plague us into adulthood will portend our destiny.

In *The Odyssey*, Circe, Greek goddess of magic, restores Odysseus and his men to their authentic state: pigs. Hermes releases the spell, but only so that Odysseus can fulfill his destiny: the circular journey: the loop. Circe's name is derived from the Greek verb *kirkoô,* meaning to secure with rings or to hoop. Myth, too, tethers us to our primary sources of understanding.

I drink from the hose though my mother tells me not to. The water is so cold. It tastes like truth. It's merely satiation. Please don't tell me— Let me drink.

SNOW

SNOW IS AMPLE AND FRANK

It has a roundness of being. It presses us into its breast.

Others object. Snow is not spherical, they say. They characterize snow's inner voluptuousness in terms of the Mandelbrot set.

Geography and Minimalism were born of a desire for relief. Snow continues to relieve both geographers and minimalists of their trashcans and their grief.

Snow blots out the words on the strip mall marquee. It has no past. It speaks of no prior experience. Its résumé is a blank sheet of paper.

Despite its institutional commitment to unfinished durational works, snow appears in sparkling completion, unexpectedly, like a screensaver.

We find ourselves swollen under snow's hypnotic power. Like chicks swollen in our shells, we must scrape through its opacity to release ourselves.

On an antenna on a rooftop of snow, a sparrow is spherical. Its shadow is a circle. The shortest distance from my eye to the bird is a curved line. Soul is the quantum point that blinks alive in both of us, at the same time.

DESERTS

BAALBEK, LEBANON

I

The desert begins by running away. It is the object that flees. Almost immediately, it is distant, elsewhere. The desert landscape, its elements, their spatial dimensions, distort in the scree. The desert horizon is a productive flow through which the landscape rises and sinks.

The sudden wind is rigid as granite.

The sudden wind is a limit.

2

A Saudi woman in full hijab stands on the stairs of the Temple of Bacchus. She wears both abaya and niqab and over them, she has draped an additional black silk jilbab. Not the mesh grille burqa, the burqa I've seen on the internet and on the cover of *National Geographic*. The woman's silk is a thin sheen that balloons in the wind as though she were afloat in a bubble of oil.

"the women of Ansar came out as if they had crows over their heads"

The Arabic word *hijab* can be translated into *veil, screen, barrier, cover, mantle, curtain, drapes*. It can also be translated as *partition, division, divider, wall*.

But why? I am American; I have no answer.

"There is no compulsion in religion," says my guide, a Lebanese schoolteacher dressed in a bright pink polo and khakis, her hair coiffed and clipped but visible. Rules of a religion become self-evident to the devout.

The Saudi woman stands above us on the stairs of the Temple of Bacchus. She smooths her silk bubble with a black-gloved hand. I can't see her face but I can tell by her posture that she is very beautiful. Her husband joins her. He wears a white turban that curls to the sky like vanilla soft serve.

I carry my compulsions to the desert. I carry my compulsions in metaphor's suitcase. I see what I am.

There is no compulsion in the desert. We surround the desert with compulsions, invest in it our limitations, but limits are accidents.

3

Never does a desert appear as a complete field. A desert falls off its edges.

There is a dizziness in the desert: the vertigo of the outlier.

The desert knows no bounds in "this space that has its being in you." (Rilke)

4

In the severe light, I play the black keys of the Temple of Jupiter, hopping along the spears of shadows of columns that slice black the stone road. I kneel on the road, press my cheek against a shadow's path of least resistance. The shadow is Roman. It will not last. It will return again tomorrow.

I write:

> *In the severe light, I play*
> *the black keys*
>
> *of the Temple of Jupiter,*
> *hopping along the spears*
>
> *of shadows of columns*
> *that slice black the stone road.*
>
> *I kneel on the road, press*
> *my cheek against a shadow's*
>
> *path of least resistance. The shadow*
> *is Roman. It will not last.*
>
> *It will return again tomorrow.*

5

Concerning the contradictory characteristics of the desert (hot and cold, dead and alive, barren and fertile, frenetic and still, boundary and center, origin and end, dark and bright, void and swollen with meaning), our compulsion to volley between them: Dunes are parabolas. Their traversable patches lure us to peaks of hot volumes and bleak repose.

The desert's fragment pins us in its untenable bounds.

When I flew to the desert, I thought I wanted to flee the world, but what I wanted was to pull its edges up around me.

6

The natural desert is not silent.

It was in the American suburbs' anechoic chambers that I learned the silent
    insult of being typified.

I learned the rules: Flashy accumulated wealth is a low-class woman's way
    of demonstrating her equality.

I learned the rules: I collected my indecisive moments, my hesitations,
    my *I-should-have-saids* and recast them as
    transitions.

I rebelled against the myth of attainable perfection,
    substituting one of transcendent,
    authentic, freedom-granting
    destruction.

I flew to Beirut.

7

"Why is there no young desert?" the Harvard-educated Genius Man Poet says.

Oh, there is.

The young desert seethes with light

8

In the desert there is scarcity.

At a roadside bakery, I stuff myself with rose-infused syrup on rose-dusted cream puffs, dried rose buds in rose-petal tea. I'm a car: I'm full, I'm empty, I'm full, I'm empty. I can't tell if I'm emotional-eating or if I'm honest-to-God starving. An American, I'm supposed to know the difference. In America, there is a difference.

The people who eat aren't always the hungriest people.

The highway is lined with Stonehenges that were meant to rise into luxury malls and condominium complexes but money and labor died in the war.

An abandoned complex has sheets for windows.

It isn't abandoned.

9

We park on the sand at Tyre. My guide shows me where to walk on the Roman road, past the open graves barred with rebar, the exposed femurs and clavicles. Alone, I navigate the coliseum's outer rings and ascend onto the floor of the ampitheatre. Its stones are the color of weak tea and stale biscuits. Air so still, my exhale is epic.

I hear my eyelids close and blink open.

The silence sounds like a faraway crowd.

> *I will make you a bare rock*
> *You shall be a place for the spreading of nets*
>
> —*Ezekiel 26:14*

10

"Deserts possess a particular magic, since they have exhausted their own futures," writes J.G. Ballard. "Anything erected there, a city, a pyramid, a motel, stands outside time."

The desert has no discrete doorway. We cannot mark the moment at which we enter or will exit its stage. The desert's only measurements of *hello, goodbye* are parts A and B of its second act: sunset, sunrise. An object constructed in the desert gains potency, matures into prophecy, as it method-acts the tireless progression of future to past using only the film of its shadow: *come here, come back.*

11

When the sun sets, we drive back to Beirut.

We meet a pair of teachers for dinner at a balcony café downtown. No one eats. I order ice cream. Three perfect scoops: *rose, rose, rose.*

> *The Roman gladiator's promise*
> *is not just*
>
> *to kill*
> *but to gore*
>
> *the hell*
> *out of silence*

12

In the darkness beyond the balustrade, titanium lights have been artfully arranged to highlight the petrified forest of an archeological dig. The trees are pillars. The sprigs are fiber optic wires. A white Persian cat springs onto the illuminated base of a pedestal and challenges my stare.

I ask the teachers *what's being unearthed?*

The tank treads and heavy artillery exhumed an ancient city.

Will it be preserved? I ask.

They laugh.

The city is under the city. If we want to preserve the old, we'll have to tear down the new.

13

A fever in my skin: Cannot open my eyes: Can't even rise to peek through the blinds. I'm pink as a Western sunset. Room service delivers ice cubes and cotton napkins. I slide the ice over my eyelids, cheeks, and neck; the melt pools in the notches of my clavicles. My hands are roasted rock Cornish game hens. I spread the napkins over my thighs.

The desert is the middle. The middle of *fitness.*

At dusk, I need air. I dress in gray linen, a loose black cotton hoodie, and black sunglasses that wilt violet in the sunlight. I tug the hood over my hair, over

Quinacridone Gold
Caput Mortuum
Tyrian Purple

Outside the hotel, I pass the pockmarked facades of ancestral homes, their classical Arabic filigree sandblasted by shrapnel, their

Cinnabar
Red Fiesta Ware
Bone Char, or Ivory Black

I walk until I reach the Holiday Inn, one of the first fronts in a war staged in armored vehicles, commando units charging the lobbies, ballrooms, and elevator shafts of the Phoenicia InterContinental, the Palm Beach, the Excelsior, the Alcazar, the St. Georges, the unfinished Hilton Beirut Habtoor Grand and Murr Tower as bullets sizzled from rooftops and windows.

The Battle of the Hotels

The sun has set behind the Holiday Inn's desiccated tower. A black cloud smokes in the blue milk dusk. *It burns, it burns*—then I realize—*there's no fire.*

The hotel is full of bats.

PALO ALTO, CA

I

What I saw was the husk of time

White dawn in palm fronds;
     white noise of a leaf blower

clearing the parking lot of eucalyptus;
     white cream in my coffee.

         I go to the desert
     and I return to the desert. Jet-lagged

and up at a pale hour to soothe myself with coffee, Rilke, *The New York Times,*
the needle on a record (Bonnie Prince Billy's *I See a Darkness*).

California is running out of water.

Wildfires have blackened the hills of Oakland and Malibu.

     Time discards its husk

       The husk is us

2

"All art is the result of one's having been in danger," writes Rilke, "of having gone through an experience all the way to the end, where no one can go any further."

In my hardcover Laboratory Notebook (which is, with its silver embossing, blue college rule, red memory ribbon, an American fetish object), I write: *Here, the million volts: Here, the Continental breakfast: If I give up music for anything, let it be poetry.*

I load up my PC.

Overnight, J has posted to Livejournal: *You know how when you're driving somewhere new and you don't know where you're going? You know how just when you're just about to stop and turn around because you think you've gone in the wrong direction—how if you just go a little farther, you're there? There must be an algorithm for this.*

*mood: *~bashful~**

3

(This was approximately half a decade
before everyone had GPS.
Crazy Town's "Butterfly"

was still on the radio and I
was still listening to the radio.

In fact, I'd put on
Bonnie Prince Billy precisely
because Crazy Town's "Butterfly"

was on the radio and it was 5 AM.)
(Why was I in California.
New York was my home.

Would I ever make it back. These weren't questions. They were geodes. Stones in
my wallet. But this morning, I'd decided. The desert had decided. The radio, the
leafblower, the eucalyptus had decided.)

4

I click out of LJ and type *CheapTickets.com*. I type *N Y C* and select *1 person, any
time, any date, any airport.* Error.

I redirect to AA.com, the website of American Airlines. Error.

I check my Ethernet cable. Refresh. Time-out. Not even a 404— whiteout. Error.

CNN.com to browse the news. Again, time-out.

A rectangle and "alt= "

AMERICAN FLAG
AMERICAN FLAG
AMERICAN FLAG
AMERICAN FLAG

5

To say *a desert of information* and mean *a lack of information* isn't fair to the desert. Nor is it fair to the data.

Information wants to be free of earthbound beings.

Air, data exhaled into data; data, air exhaled into air.

> *Like data, a cactus*
> *secretes the husk that defines it.*
> *The husk that is shucked*
> *like an error*
> *when a thirty surveyor*
> *seeks data in the desert.*

6

It seems like a flag, a symbol of a unified whole, but *to seem* implies a split between reality and its depiction. It appears as an expression of national unity. I know it is a disaster. Its error is the message. The "alt=" is the message: *ALTERNATE UNDEFINED*. There is no substitute offered for what fails to arrive.

A static image in a dynamic field, the gif's hieroglyphic, its lossy format was engineered to reduce transfer time, increasing broadcasted iterations.

Is the message.

I prepare myself for Occam's razor.

I prepare myself for an increasingly broadcasted narrative that will be true to those who define it as true.

7

I watch myself
watch the day
          affix itself to its borders
                    as a rear view mirror clenches a sky.

No dial tone, my ear pressed against the network's hollow. I can't tolerate the TV screen, its blue glow: In spite of television's violent artifice, this horror is the actual horror, spliced into the morning. The implosion's ominous sincerity, the branded troposphere, sundowns to a major coda until all that's left is its loop.

I drive to the hill, hike five sine waves of yellow grass. Three crows at the foot of a satellite dish. Here, the narrative adapts: Horror's thrill will now depend, not on a suspension of disbelief, but on belief itself. Belief in the actual. Belief that *it happens*.

#nofilter

8

There are no ideals in nature.
There is no ideal daisy.
There is no ideal evergreen.
As soon as a plant achieves fitness,
fitness itself modulates
to suit the shifting environment.
Ideal is a human thing.
Humans pluck the petals
from the ideal
she-loves-me daisy.
Humans bicker in the street
over the ideal
Christmas tree.
Ideal is aspirational,
but plants do not aspire
to "harder, better, faster, stronger,"
land, plastics, oil, fun. Ideal
assumes permanence. Ideal
assumes a deep river runs
continuously inside of us.
Chomsky called it "deep grammar."

Insisted that two things said differently
could harbor the same meaning.
But a phrase's form
is especially relevant
when speaking of murder
and History. "The men
are leaping from the building"
is less ideal
than "the nations shed their men,"
depending on the circumstance
though both express
the same grotesque. There
is no ideal description. There
is no everlasting
daisy.
There is no evergreen
evergreen. We
pluck only its depiction. Crown
it with the Angel
of History. Its boughs,
analytics.
They are already empty.

9

My suitcase in the trunk of my Honda Accord, I drive to Death Valley with only
my houseplants to keep me company.

Eight miles outside of Death Valley National Park, road debris gnashes my right front tire. On the gravel shoulder, I remember how green lightning flashed over Manhattan, how the rod on top of the World Trade Center channeled and discharged that energy. Where would the lightning go? I eat a roll of Mentos. AAA arrives and tows me 45 miles into the sunset to buy a new rubber hole.

The sky is an amethyst. On the phone, the ranger at the park-run hotel reception says she'll wait up, take my time, drive safe, go slow, but my foot is heavy on the pedal.

From the road, the hotel pool is a square-cut sapphire on black velvet.

I carry my metaphors; I carry.

10

The Bible on the faux-wood nightstand is split open to Ecclesiastes:

> *The sun also rises, and the sun goes down,*
> *And hastens to the place where it arose.*

11

Finally, between polyester sheets, the network loads:

K answers her phone. She tells me she spent all day on the Brooklyn Bridge, shuffling home as charred paper snowed.

12

The moon is a cue ball on the desert's black billiards table.

NEVADA TEST SITE, NV

I

So many ways to begin.
There is History:

I am American.
I prefer the movie:

The Conqueror, a western starring John Wayne as Genghis Khan, was filmed downwind from the craters. The cast and crew spent weeks on location while Operation Upshot–Knothole exploded eleven aboveground atomic shells into the atmosphere. Producer Howard Hughes later shipped local dirt to Hollywood in order to match the terrain in studio re-shoots.

Out of the 220-person cast and crew, 91 died of cancer, including director Dick Powell (lymphoma) and John Wayne (stomach cancer).

Log line:

In an ancient world, a warlord battles a rival tribe. He defeats his enemies within and without, and is crowned the ULTIMATE RULER.

I am an American.
I prefer the movie.

2

We check into The Luxor.

Our tour begins in the morning, early, 5 AM. We slip past King Tut's Tomb and into the casino to play quarter slots. The hall sounds like a children's choir intoning around a harmonium. A shimmy of jingle bells. I win $2.75, which I use to purchase a Starbucks mint mocha at the MGM Grand.

Out on the strip, the Luxor Sky Beam, a pole of light, blares into the atmosphere. Curved mirrors in the hotel roof channel the xenon glow into one bright ray that can be seen from Los Angeles airspace on a clear winter night.

Early Luxor promotional materials claim that the beam is so bright you can use it to read a newspaper ten miles above the hotel if you are suspended in the air.

This fact is unverifiable.

Now, our drones and satellites scan our targets' retinas with absolute clarity.

3

Luxor, modern

incarnation of Thebes, gateway

to the Valley of the Kings,

scored into hours

no one was intended to relieve /

Blue crystal chimney

pressure vaporized

the deep grammar / What

do we prepare for

that we have not already devoured?

4

On a bus with black mirror windows, our guide introduces himself as a former test site meteorologist and a Republican. Cell phones and cameras will be confiscated. The man I mistakenly love beeps off his phone and stashes it in an inner pocket. I fear, not for his phone, but for a poem. I worry it will rot in the bud. Before I left for the desert, a Man Poet scolded me for writing about the desert. He told me I should never set out to write. He told me I should never set out to write *about*. That poems are not *about*. That poems should be free from *about*. He wilfully misunderstood me.

Free is a luxury.
The privilege you need

to claim to write
nothing
is as louche as a Porsche.

Some poets believe
that poems are free

as water lost in water is free
from materiality—

But the idea is to be *free of*
not *free from*

and the truth is, poems
are objects in materiality's *FREE* box
and poets are pickers.

We choose
forms
based on what the universe
has left out for us.

Sometimes those poems are poems.
Sometimes those poems are genocides.
Sometimes those poems are deserts.

5

The bus crawls past a chain-link livestock pen used to detain protesters before transferring them to the state police or to the FBI, depending. The pen of Rebecca Solnit's *Savage Dreams*. The pen that we are persuaded, through point-of-view identification with the hero, to deem necessary in the multimillion-dollar blockbuster movie. The pen is the tank of Damian Hirst's *The Impossibility of Death in the Mind of Someone Living*. The pen is *formal constraint,* a machine, the same repurposed mechanism that conceptual art strip-mined of meaning. Like Kenneth Goldsmith, the Test Site has composed a sonnet.

(The Man Poet told me I should sit on the lawn and recite James Wright. He had the privilege of hollering *I have wasted my life!* in a hammock on sabbatical; I had three wage jobs.

(What is the economy of poetry.

(Why are some poets worth more than others.

(Why must my labor be divorced from my work.)

4

Moon-Landing Deniers: They know this desert.

Once, at the beginning of the Aughts, I read on a conspiracy blog that the moon landing was filmed on the atomic craters.

The blog (Geocities, defunct) didn't call itself a "conspiracy blog." This is the adult in me speaking.

Later, I heard a rumor that Neil Armstrong and Buzz Aldrin used the atomic craters to practice moonwalking.

This information is also unverifiable.

5

The desert is unverifiable because the desert is erasure.

Not the natural desert, not the desert of cholla, paloverde, and sahuaro. I mean the technological desert. As I write this, post-Aughts, the Nevada Test Site's doors are open, courtesy of Google's satellites.

I Google *Nevada Test Site map* and servers produce a rendering of sand swathe and rectangular settlements. I click on a blue bubble pin and a pop-up informs me:

> *Area 51 / Groom Lake*
> *The airbase that you see here does not exist.*

6

In all symbols of power and control, there is erasure. *For instance, the head of a bear:*

In English heraldry the beheading is done horizontally under the neck, which is itself not lost, whereas in Scottish heraldry the practice is for the head to be detached from the body, isolated without the neck—

Blazonry, the language of heraldry. The profession

grants

heraldic linens. An alias

ammonia: *reagent. doctorate.* What ascends lavender

GO

in porcelain, there are acacia [NO keys]   What tonsure:

harmonium

marion

wingspan

peonies

lily lock   *egg colonnades*

shoshone

suede Orchis

reaper fox
        honey "Test"

    and "Proving"

daffodils   *Dow*   *Mons*

   cavities

   / Formica

choked with preparations

    tower   *Lockheed*   *garnish*

easy   *good*   *square*   *flank*   *GALILEO*

then

    axis

WHAT ENDURES FOR REAL

liminality

disobedience

7

In power, *erasure* signifies obliteration.

In poems, *erasure* signifies remains.

8

Forklifts fit a trench with waste cartons; diggers dust the cartons with sand.

The meteorologist informs us that the cartons are gold-lined. Gold is stable. Gold is the BPA-laced tin can of the nuclear waste industry.

The man I mistakenly love pops open a bag of Sun Chips.

He says: *We're burying something that's still alive. How do you feel about that.*

I say: *I understand the zombie.*

He says: *Look where Marie Curie led us.*

I say: *Radioactivity was discovered by a woman. The bomb was built by men.*

9

I don't need a war.

I have nothing to defend.

10

When I'm finally tall and strong enough, my grandfather lets me tip the hourglass. This is what we do: We watch Benny Hill and eat maraschino cherries trapped in chocolate and tip the hourglass. The sand streams, fast and fine, from the top into the bottom of its container. I don't question its quickness. I don't question its shape or its color, its formless voluptuousness.

How do you stop the sand from flowing? my grandfather asks, and I turn the hourglass onto its side.

He laughs. Can you do it without turning it onto its side?

I try to use my mind. I will the sand to stasis, but the sand drizzles into the bottom teardrop.

The trickle, he says, is gravity. Gravity is why we trip and fall.

I know this direction: down. Down seems so arbitrary. Outside on the lawn, I lie on my back and imagine I'm falling into the sky.

Why can't I stop the sand from falling? The suspension of sand has the smugness of knowing. Like the girls at church with swimming pools. Like the mothers who look at me like I'm beetle on a begonia.

I draw close to the glass. I watch the sand's topography. When the hourglass is fresh, the sand's surface is level. Then the surface puckers into a funnel like the black tiled wishing well at the mall, like a waffle cone, like a construction paper bugle. The sand is a white hole. There is a secret trapped in its fact.

How many flips until the sky goes black? my grandfather asks.

I flip and flip through the sunset, but the sky never goes black. The horizon is tangerine, then deep blue, the fruit of a bruise.

Standing at the lip of the Sedan crater, I think of the hourglass.

My grandfather says: It measures time.

What is my half-life.

What is the half-life of time.

11

Leaving Las Vegas, we drive past Red Rock Canyon National Conservation Area. He pulls to the side of the road. He wants to fuck in the front seat so that passing cars can see us. The sky is periwinkle and the moon is a cold white ass.

> *The closer I come to my own erasure*
> *the stronger my work's urge*
>
> *to story, the stronger my work's will*
> *to theme. I must be careful.*
>
> *If my language is obscure*
> *I'll vanish in its steam.*

We take out our notebooks. He scrawls: *The woman was so mannish, he almost mistook her for Thomas Pynchon.* I write:

> *no one tells the cardinal*
>
> *there are no cardinals*
>
> *in the desert*

12

> When I say: *The desert is an erasure,*
>
> I mean: *It resists.*

I mean: *It is the last legible word*

where the world

has swallowed its resources.

LUXOR

I

"An immense space-time unites all things, but only by introducing between them the distances of a Sahara," writes Deleuze.

Exhibit A: *immense*

I've endeavored and failed to exclude the adjective from my manuscript. The adjective would like to lend a specificity to the sand, to couple the sand with a feeling or a dimension, but sand and adjectives have nothing in common.

If we experience the desert's intensity as *immense*, it is because we contrast our brief duration within its mirage of limitlessness to the geologic age of a grain of sand.

The wind in the sand is harmonically indecisive. The desert is more fluid than the tonal paradigms it disenchants.

2

The sand stands at odds with my desire to use it as an exemplar of both economy and ethic. My awkward American questions:

Is it possible to visit the desert without colonizing the desert?

How is the desert invented? Who benefits?

3

An excavation, the Nile has little to do with the expression of its depth, its sculptural arm.

A river flows through it.

A river of movement.

4

Writing of movement, my text elides collision with my spoken body. Collusion?

Sand whips itself into sound.

This is also a definition of the cosmos: Sound whips itself into sand.

5

Movement has a memory, and because of its melody, is included in a classification of earworms along with pop tunes and curses.

I'll never forget the way you pinched my ear. I'll never forget how you told me you liked my pigtails, you liked what came out of my mouth. I'll never forget how the boys on the hill threw a brick through the window. I'll never forget when you called the waiter a kike, a cockfucker. I'll never forget the Easter card with your cripple's handwriting: I hate your mother and I hope she dies. I'll never forget when you said I was a fat tomato. I'll never forget how you told me

DON'T PUT YOUR TRUST IN INSTITUTIONS

6

Sand's premise:

You'll forget

NEVER FORGET NEVER FORGET NEVER FORGET
NEVER FORGET NEVER FORGET NEVER FORGET
NEVER FORGET NEVER FORGET NEVER FORGET
NEVER FORGET NEVER FORGET NEVER FORGET
NEVER FORGET NEVER FORGET NEVER FORGET
NEVER FORGET NEVER FORGET NEVER FORGET
NEVER FORGET NEVER FORGET NEVER FORGET
NEVER FORGET NEVER FORGET NEVER FORGET
NEVER FORGET NEVER FORGET NEVER FORGET
NEVER FORGET NEVER FORGET NEVER FORGET
NEVER FORGET NEVER FORGET NEVER FORGET
NEVER FORGET NEVER FORGET NEVER FORGET
NEVER FORGET NEVER FORGET NEVER FORGET
NEVER FORGET NEVER FORGET NEVER FORGET
NEVER FORGET NEVER FORGET NEVER FORGET
NEVER FORGET NEVER FORGET NEVER FORGET
NEVER FORGET NEVER FORGET NEVER FORGET
NEVER FORGET NEVER FORGET NEVER FORGET
NEVER FORGET NEVER FORGET NEVER FORGET
NEVER FORGET NEVER FORGET NEVER FORGET
NEVER FORGET NEVER FORGET NEVER FORGET
NEVER FORGET NEVER FORGET NEVER FORGET
NEVER FORGET NEVER FORGET NEVER FORGET
NEVER FORGET NEVER FORGET NEVER FORGET
NEVER FORGET NEVER FORGET NEVER FORGET
NEVER FORGET NEVER FORGET NEVER FORGET
NEVER FORGET NEVER FORGET NEVER FORGET
NEVER FORGET NEVER FORGET NEVER FORGET
NEVER FORGET NEVER FORGET NEVER FORGET
NEVER FORGET NEVER FORGET NEVER FORGET

7

I'll never forget my mother dancing, singing—"she wears her sunglasses at night"—the road's yellow line a ballet barre, then a tightrope. This was the 1980s; there weren't many cars on the road. My mother always wanted to be a dancer, but her favorite teacher died of Lou Gehrig's.

Why couldn't she find another teacher? Or just—*go dance*. I couldn't imagine not having the will to claw my way out of a lack of supervision.

I was a different beast. No, I was the same beast, raised in a different pasture, fed different feed. I didn't have the burden of caring for myself and for me.

8

When I went to the desert, I expected to be free of the powers of pop tunes. I expected to be free of the powers of curses and gravity. I expected to be free of the thigh gap, free of crow's feet and laugh lines. No longer locked in my weight, secretary to my senses.

My body's dark loaf, elongated shadow, a whole note on a sheet of staff paper,

about to be lifted.

9

It is unfair, to say: *Having made a desert of.*

When I went to the desert, I expected nihilism. But the desert demands we reject the easy negative and learn instead to play the polyphony that must be played with one hand.

10

O Valley

of Kings

You buried

your muses

11

In Ancient Egyptian, the word *Nefertiti* means "the beautiful one has come."

If the future is in the past, let it be from Luxor.

Let it be made of mysteries that cannot be exhumed without raising the dead.

LOS ANGELES, CA

In the beautiful air-conditioned home
of the biofuel engineer
and the installation artist,
I write: "Indistinct seep of habitat
with no beginning, no end"
thinking of the harems of monarch butterflies
crossing deserts to migrate en masse
Bouquets of butterflies hanging from rafters
like bundles of peppers and roses
in unexpected settlements
due to cold winds and airplane traffic
I think of Los Angeles
I think of the hill
I climbed late night in Echo Park
to fetch my guitar from the car
How the animal parts of me,
my primal brain stem,
the invisible ears that slant atop my head
pricked up
like solar panels
How the invisible eyes that hover above my hair
blinked open
like lighthouse beacons
How the invisible heart that beats above my chest
like heat floats above sand
was a quivering jelly
How I saw them before I saw them

How curious they were,
lined up in the street to question me
along the cars and the eucalyptus, the garbage and the recycling,
like concrete garden gnomes
in a semi-circle,
the wolves

ALBUQUERQUE, NM

I

I went to the desert and it rained, and it rained, and it rained.

We chase a storm from Phoenix to Albuquerque. Lightning on all sides as we enter the city. Purple billows over the buildings. Forks of light. A dark smear fizzles over the sunset. *Virga*—the rain evaporates before it hits the ground. The steam rises back into the sky like the cloud's ladling its tears and drinking them.

2

In Santa Fe, I walk the railroad tracks from A's house to the grocery store. Hot gravel, signposts: *shunt, faught.* Hear a word, say it, repeat it. The process of becoming an individual is repetitive. It involves repeating one's movements, one's words, until the motion, the word becomes indistinguishable from the person.

The process of individuation is also performative. Becoming an individual requires us to draw from the performances of others.

The sun comes out. I wear S's black wide-brimmed hat, sunglasses, my neck and hair tied swaddled in her red bandana.

The most profound affections are banalities.

3

We play two shows: Santa Fe and Albuquerque; then have two days off until Amarillo, Norman, St. Joseph, and on and through the middle of the country: Des Moines, Chicago, Columbus, Cleveland, Pennsylvania, then home to Brooklyn. We'd started in Los Angeles.

We stay with B and R at the Dome. We can't make it out to the geodesic homestead our first night in New Mexico because the rain has washed out the road (the stay at A's in town, the errands, the tracks) but rain dries fast in the desert. The Dome is located somewhere between Santa Fe and Taos. From the front porch, you see buttes. BLM land. There's a dirt road and another dirt road and then a dirt drive and animal-worn paths that cross a system of arroyos.

B tells us how R's wife once tried to cross an arroyo during a storm. She misjudged the strength of the current and nearly lost her right hand when she was swept downstream and grabbed a barbed-wire fence.

In the desert, heat and light and cut are pure. I could almost forget the words *self-mythologize, fabricate scarcity.*

4

My dad died sixteen days before Albuquerque. I don't want to tell anyone. I want it to be a secret. Back in New York, someone I trusted had robbed me. I don't want to talk about this, either. I want it to be a secret, too. I also want to shout it loud, but I'm shamed by things that shouldn't shame me.

What is shame. What is cut.

(Leslie Jamison writes: "intellect swells around hurt.")

5

All year, I've been making work about the sunset. I've been writing songs about ghosts, poems and essays about women, art, color, cuts. *The world doesn't need any more photographs of sunsets.* Sometimes it seems our cultural institutions only support women who write about cunts. Women who get naked. Who have good bodies. Who take good portraits. Women who know how to pose. I'm tired of third-wave feminism. Sometimes it seems all artists must be body artists. I'm tired of second-wave feminism. I don't want to wear pearls. I want to be me, unkempt me, sexless me, genderless me, me with my frizzy hair in faded cotton.

Outside the Dome, sprawled across an inflatable mattress, my hamstrings and shoulders ill with ache (the meat kind of ache), I write:

In the sunset, there is no cultural past.
In the sunset, there is no sex.
Note: in the sunset—not—at sunset.
Time is cultural. So is sex. So is moment.
One is receptive to the sunset
the moment it appears.
One receives the sunset
as its angle of declension lessens. In this way,
the sunset is parliament

to all forms of measured loss.
If there be a philosophy of the sunset,
it must appear and reappear
in adherence to the freshness of its image.
If I take on the burden of writing a philosophy
of the sunset, I
must appear and reappear in adherence
to the freshness
of my limerence. Freshness: a kind of cleanliness,
a kind of death.
If I take on the burden of writing philosophy,
the language
must be genderless.
At midnight, it is hard to know
at what depth the philosophy
will reverberate, how long
it will be until it is extinguished.
At noon, its archetype sleeps.
I am in between. It is morning.

6

Chimayo is a site of miracles. I'm still not sure what *miracle* means, but I have a plastic baggie from when I bought a ghost bead bracelet from a two-spirit person at a reservation gas station. The baggie is tiny. The bracelet is tiny; I have child-sized wrists. I fill the baggie full of holy dirt. It looks like a bag of heroin. *I could get addicted to miracles,* I think. Couldn't anybody.

I feel like I need a miracle. I do know miracles. The miracle of friendship. The miracle of crossing a continent. A while ago, I read an article that decried the lack of female road narratives. Like this is something that women don't just do: Get in the car and drive. Book shows and readings in places they've never been, show up, make friends. Watch sand dry from the head of a butte or from the gut of an alluvial fan. Seems like I've been a punk for so long that there's no other way for me to live.

But driving can't cleanse me of my cuts.
Driving can't cleanse me of my gender.
Driving can't cleanse me of my status anxiety.

7

Joan Didion writes about the desert twice in *The White Album*, first in "Holy Water" and again in "At the Dam." She speaks of a "reverence for water" but what she's really talking about is power.

She says: "I wanted to drain Quail myself"; "I wanted to produce"; "pull it down and then refill it"; "I wanted to shut down all flow"; "I wanted to stay"; "I wanted to be the one"; "I want it still."

At the Hoover Dam, she steps across the star map, the illustration of the sidereal revolution of the equinox, that "fixes forever" the date the dam was dedicated. She writes: "I thought of it then, with the wind whining and the sun dropping behind a mesa with the finality of a sunset in space. Of course that was the image I had seen always, seen it without quite realizing what I saw, a dynamo finally free of man, splendid at last in its absolute isolation, transmitting power and releasing water to a world where no one is."

What Joan wants is power.

8

From Wikipedia's Dynamo (disambiguation) page:

- Dynamo, *a magnetic device originally used as an electric generator*

- Dynamo theory, *a theory relating to magnetic fields of celestial bodies*

- Solar dynamo, *the physical process that generates the Sun's magnetic field*

The word *dynamo* comes from the Greek *dynamis*, meaning "power."

Dictionary.com offers two definitions:

1. an electric generator,
2. an energetic, hardworking, forceful person.

I think: *You became your dynamo. You became immortal. As immortal as the sun's archetype in literature's brief duration.*

9

In Santa Fe, I walk the tracks to the yoga studio. The biological process of becoming a body is repetitive. The social process of becoming a body in space is also repetitive. It's also performative. In yoga, you're supposed to repeat but you're not supposed to perform. Not in the way we think of performing, like on a stage, or in a movie. But I do perform, in ways I'm proud of and in ways I'm not.

I once left a man after he pointed to an American Apparel advertisement and said: "This is what you'd look like if you actually exercised." I escaped a man who said, after closing a browser of bondage porn: "I prefer a Japanese body."

They knew what to say to enrage me. But still, I can't help but want to look good. Their words make me eat less, move harder.

The yoga teacher is an older woman who tells us she used to ride horses. She corrects my arms, coaxing them further and further from my core. She whispers: "Take up more space."

From California to the New York island.

> *Solar dynamo,*
> *use the heat from your salutations to generate*
> *a magnetic field*

> *Dynamo theory,*
> *remember the attractive and repulsive qualities of*
> *your celestial vibrations*

Dynamo,
when you twist, an electric current pulses
outwards from your heart

MARGIN DESERT

I

According to Twitter Analytics, my image of my aloe plant has done much better for itself than my image of an alpaca in a thorn sward.

> "Desert succulents are known for their sturdy forms and resilient temperaments. Aloe vera continues to bloom long after it is abandoned. "

> Keywords: *desert, succulent, aloe, plant, sunburn, remedy*

2

I am an image doctor. I retouch, caption, and keyword for a stock photography agency. My craft will linger on in search engine optimized memory. I loiter on melodramatic gestures such as *long after it has been abandoned* the way I loitered in parking lots as a teenager. How long is *long*? How abandoned is *abandoned*? Why do I write *Desert succulents* when *succulents* would be sufficient? Why the impulse to fill a page?

Advertising fills its page. Advertising aspires to eliminate the boundary between the fantasy and the actual.

Prose requires a firm border. How much space from the text to the edge of the world? It depends on content, tone, and genre.

Poetry accommodates the widest margins of all.

How little can I write before the page blinks open?

3

There is only a millimeter of glass between me and the virtual world. My iPhone case casts the illusion of a durable rubber margin, but when the phone blinks on, I enter one world and exit another.

I mean, both worlds open in me. There is one world.

Our dogs guard my mother as she sleeps on the rock, one dog on each side, alert as sphinxes. My mother is retiring; she will soon be moving. I remember our first move: *red house, wood deck, a rock reaching out onto water.*

A different dog: a dog named *Chopin.*

When my phone is off, the glass is black glass. When the phone is on, the glass disappears.

I use a warming filter, a filter called *Rise*, to convey the heat of the stones, the immediate presence and transmutable quality of that heat. *If there be a God, if there be gods, let them be made of #stones.*

Let them be made of the water's clock
Let the clock rid me

4

I lie on the hot rock as though it is a body, my body, a phantom. This is less about the haunted erotic and more about the actual, the real, presence, materiality.

Our dogs are named *Aleph* and *Balthazar*.

The most honorable thing one can aspire to be is a dog on a rock out of water.

The dog is text; the rock is margin; the water is the world. Or is it: The water is text; the rock is margin; the dog is world.

5

Music is an expanse.

An expanse with no margin.

I cannot recall my first sound, though the womb enclosed me like the hum of a room painted a primary color.

When two tones ring close enough together in time, they are perceived as one.

A purely imagined tone is elusive; hummed, a tone is born.

Hum? Did I mean the moon's pull on the future of rhythm—

> *Aleph, my littlest infinity*

> *Balthazar, my wise*
> *bitch*

> *We're binge-watching the moon*
> *tonight*

> *We're watching the moon*
> *get fat and rich*

5

The wind's ripples in the dunes, the dunes' ripples on the tectonic plate, the scrub brush's undulations in the gust, the regular, repeated scatter of creatures, their signatures inscribed at the bottom of the trench.

6

I would like to substitute *questions* for *dogs* and *rocks* and *stones*.

The generality *question* cannot be easily search engine optimized. You need a quality, linked to a noun or a verb, to pop you to the top of a search.

So much effort to signify. To access the actual with the help of a signifier's signifier. And down the chain of command.

I tap my phone, connect to my history. The physical proximity to progress feeds my impulse to contribute to it.

A timeline is personal.

But I have done enough for the day, retracing my steps from water to gravel.

I tell myself a glacier can't rewrite its trough.

Once, we were glaciers. Only a film of time separates ice from hand.

7

Once, in northern latitudes, I overheard the bellow of a widening glacial rift.

I heard trombones piped through a shaft; the isolated low frequencies of William Basinski's *Disintegration Loops*; the bottom octave of the Mellotron my father, high, smashed a kitchen window to take from our house late one January night.

What I heard was the stomach of time.

8

The value of a day lies in its isolation. When is a day more valued than when it has been set aside? When a day is set aside, it grows walls. Its vessel is suspended between other days that churn with capital's gearshifts. An empty day is a refuge. An empty day's walls are spells of protection.

The value of a day also lies in its remoteness. What day is more valued than a day that has passed? A day that has passed loses its boundaries; it becomes a blurred montage of moments, light, movement, afloat in nebulous ether. A day that has passed is a beautiful ruin. It cannot escape its broken aesthetic. Why it want to?

One must step outside of the day to observe this effect. One must inhabit a future posture in order to observe the present's backward glance over the wall of the past.

In ancient times, walls were more than symbols of protection. Walls literally kept the riff-raff out. To reside inside a city's walls meant you were defined, identified, safe, defended. In the city, you rose and retired with the earth's rotation. The day's walls made the city possible. Sunrise and sunset gave a natural structure to the human dream.

Capital revised the dream. Now we rise in the dark at an alarm clock's beep. Sunset is a postcard. There is no soothing screen to which a soul might retreat. One is always under the gun. When is an hour more valued: when it is over, or when it has just begun? It depends on your ability to leverage yourself before the sun.

In ancient times, a desert was a margin, a place beyond the city's walls, beyond protection; it was also a place beyond systems of oppression. An outcast could seek comfort and refuge in the desert, if they could find water and a place to sleep. If they could build meaning into their flight. And so the desert became a place of martyrs and prophets. A martyr needs a desert narrative to draw his life like a sword; a prophet needs a desert poetry to speak what he or she foresaw.

Narrative made the desert possible, because the desert itself cannot sustain walls. All are welcome in the desert. Welcome to revel in what the desert forestalls.

9

I block my eyes in the sun. I sweat the red hour.

I stand at the threshold between anecdote and anecdote.

Narrative's hypothetical.

10

The heat of the question, the immediate presence and transmutable quality of the heat. If there be a god, let her be made of questions. Let her rid me of hypothesis, return me to premise. Who I am, I don't yet know. I lie in the question as though it were my body. The question is a phantom. This is less about the haunted, the erotic, and more about the actual, our one lone possibility in all of materiality. The most honorable thing one can aspire to do is question. Listening to water splash against the question makes me eager to surrender my life to music.

II

A wave crests
on volcanic rock

It is the shape of a question
Air bubbles

up from a crevice
The atmosphere

returns to itself
It rises like a question

SNOW

SNOW HAS A SILENT STRATEGY

I walk to the park and toss blanched peanuts to pigeons who scatter in terror from my gift. I, too, have flinched.

What comes attached? The gaze is my tether.

I gaze until there are no more details, only an arctic blue.

I gaze like a child counting to her largest number.

I gaze like a gull wrecked on land. The blur in my eye, a current, hard and cold.

I gaze and the tree is devoured by an avalanche.

I gaze into the usefulness of a white wall of washing machines.

My gaze, heavy, is full of sweetness. How the Greeks might say, *with eyes like figs.*

I eat my shadow.

I empty like a lamp shorts out.

I stream a recorded snow squall. Watching it, I am part of it.

I gaze until the screen is no longer distinguishable.

AUGHTS

I.I

In the 90s I knew a young woman who was assaulted on the steps of a university
library. She was walking home late at night, carrying a bundle of sunflowers.
Fifty sunflowers, maybe sixty, with heads as wide as salad plates. A man snuck
up behind her and pressed a pistol into her back. He raped her there, on the
library stairs. He spit on her neck. And then, as if the violence weren't enough,
he stole her sunflowers.

I watched my back when walking home late at night.

The Aughts were plagued with security.

I.2

I never hung blinds or curtains in my windows. Not until I moved into an
apartment with someone I mistakenly loved. He hated the sodium streetlights,
how they yellowed our bodies when we undressed. He didn't know that they
were called "sodium streetlights." I had to tell him what to call them. It was then
he began to use my language, my "sodium streetlights," in his stories. He adopted
my "9 o'clock blue." My favorite color of sky. He hung it over the women in his
fictions. Kidnapped women, women stuck with pins, women so mannish they
were mistaken for Thomas Pynchon.

I.3

A shared language won't save you. The pastoral won't save you. Security won't
save you.

The Aughts taught me this.

1.4

At the end of the Aughts, I met a woman who'd known a woman who rented a studio at 5 Pointz. What the building lacked in structural integrity, it made up for in cost per square foot and community. Its façade was alive with graffiti. *Wildstyle*, they call it. *Piece* for *masterpiece*. Arrows and curves and hooks and blades. Her rent was cheap because the room lacked heat, the windows lacked locks, the freight elevator permanently jammed in its shaft.

When she wasn't painting, she was kickboxing. After training, she'd hoist her bike onto one ripped shoulder and climb five floors of rusted scaffolding into her window. Every day until the day the scaffolding collapsed.

1.5

I wrote a poem:

I deboned myself.
My favorite color of frosting
was red, yellow, orange.

1.6

We are biologically attuned to tension: muscle strain, bold colors, acute angles.

My arrogant tenor, like a fleck of cadmium yellow or titanium dioxide on a canvas, diverts your attention.

What will we remember is a matter of repetition. *What will we pay attention to* is an interrogation of a landscape's ethics.

Anecdotes litter a landscape with chatter. They bedazzle the summary's flat composition, the boringness.

The reflections of smokestacks in the East River, their instability, their unwillingness to conform to the mirror's analogy or to the metaphor of the dollhouse upside down—

Aware of their conversation between what "is" and what is translated, I, too, am a shape. An anecdote, I pass through their story.

The anecdote is a spat of rain. Intellect follows later. It rises like steam.

1.7

One afternoon at the end of the Aughts, I sat on the ledge of the living room window, my Gibson J-45 in my arms. The man I mistakenly loved turned to me and said: "You're going to have to come to terms with the fact that you're never going to write anyone's favorite song."

The comment was cruel. He wanted me to feel small. He was also diminishing himself. He was a writer, a music journalist, a musician who could no longer work up the nerve to play or to read to an empty room.

The empty room was the subject of many conversations.

An empty room is a dystopian image.

An empty room is a fragment.

1.8

Through the fragment we experience the play of scale, the intensity of the trivial.

Consider the lines of difference drawn around the fragment: What is History and what is anecdote.

The streetlamp with its inverted funnel of light doesn't embody immensity, it captures it: Infinite specks of insects swirl in the cone of its glow. Its bulb has a concentrated motive, to illuminate the poem of a singular spot on the sidewalk.

I'm drawn to the fragment like a June bug. I'm attracted to its singleness, its invalidity. Its anecdotal evidence isn't valid evidence, not in the lens of science or law. Anecdotes are subjective; odds are, they've been cherry-picked. Anecdotes are gossip. They buzz with idle time.

The off-the-cuff, the spur, the smear, the slur, the stab, the microaggression, the shittiness: Each slight in its duration looms large in our emotional scenery. Like a heap of red tinsel on a January curbside.

1.9

Tell me about the incident. I want to write it.

2.1

The man I mistakenly loved wrote record reviews and artist features for music magazines before they folded or transitioned from print to online. As a reader, I preferred the web Q & A: I scanned the text; I read for difference; I wanted to discern where unrehearsed sentiments and unguarded gestures popped out of the PR-mediated copy: moments where the text seized on an artist's authentic voice: moments where things got real.

Afterwards, I'd ride my green and white Nishiki mountain bike over the Pulaski Bridge, swerve around the cemetery, pumping the pedals, pinching the brakes in a sprint from Long Island City to Maspeth. I'd thumb my disposable camera, framing the blank billboards and the pink and green dregs of Newtown Creek, imagining I was an authentic artist.

2.2

Q: How is it that some places on earth, no matter how remote, are able to present themselves as the path of least resistance?

A: I wore a black hooded sweatshirt. I purchased bulk packages of disposable cameras at my local pharmacy and kept at least one on me at all times. I wanted to remember my world in the way that I knew it, the way that I had experienced it, not in the way the media or any other artist would have me remember it years on down the road. I wanted to write my future past not as an artistic practice, but as a way of life. The Aughts were years of lost things. No, that isn't true. The Aughts were a heartbeat. They were years where anything and everything kept coming back for one last go—like an ex in a dry spell or a Labrador with a tennis ball. The decade was soaked with nostalgia like a rum cake loaded with booze. My photos, their flatness, economized my hoarding of actual items. I had a problem with hoarding in the Aughts. A yellow glass strawberry, an amethyst biscuit, a porcelain turnstile paperweight hand-cast by the owner of a very important start-up.

Q: Gateways to past selves?

A: I didn't know it then. That I was method acting.

Q: Film, like paper, has a memory.

A: I approached my body the way sculptors approach material. The way architects manipulate steel in order to extract the truth of lived experience from the inert. The narrative is alive within it; the artist must shear anything that isn't its truth. This is method acting: to excavate the depths of one's experience and discard all that isn't truly suffered. That isn't a core sample. A character study is a geology.

Q: You didn't memorize a script.

A: The script was already gone.

2.3

I'd been publishing poems in online magazines for almost a decade. Online magazines delivered exposure, but they couldn't promise pay or permanence. Magazines changed editors, underwent a redesign, and the old work would disappear. Or an account would go unpaid, the domain would expire, and the art (the data?) would evaporate.

Books, perfect-bound books, official volumes of adhesive and string and paper, connoted longevity, but I wouldn't publish a bound volume until 2012.

2.4

In the Aughts, I wrote: "The 90s were years of lost things." As soon as I'd typed the line, I knew it wasn't true.

So I typed, instead: "The Aughts were years of lost things." This wasn't true, either. It was too early in the decade for anyone characterize the decade, though I understood that everything I typed was auto-saved and logged. Gestures, public and private, captured.

Despite my draft's lack of precision, I saved the document in a folder on my desktop. I backed up the file on an external drive and emailed a copy to my Gmail.

In and after the Aughts, I am driven to *Save*.

2.5

When Google executive Vint Cerf warned that "bit rot" could lead to a "forgotten generation or even a forgotten century," I became even more determined to publish a paper book.

There is no remembrance of former things,
Nor will there be any remembrance

of things that are to come
By those who will come after

—Ecclesiastes 1:11

2.6

I wanted to be the primary source document.

I wanted to be the material.

I became a writer out of a need to remember, but I became a poet out of a need for precision. Reading poetry, I became aware of my imprecise language.

Poetry taught me *I had only my aloe plant in its clay pot to keep me company.*

2.7

A primary source embodies a specific kind of preciousness: the preciousness of little girls. I became a writer out of a desire to be adored, cajoled, delighted in, attended to, studied, revered, dismissed, and recalled, as a complex, authentic darling. My language betrayed my abject self.

My Livejournal theme was flesh-colored.

I was the subject and the object.

And like a girl, before and after and during the Aughts, I suffered a fear of being abducted.

2.8

Late night in the early Aughts, before GPS, Google Maps, and Mapquest, an unmarked car would idle at a corner near the Graham stop on the L. The driver would ask a young woman for directions. The woman, most likely new to Brooklyn, most likely a gentrifying artist (they had a type), was on her way home. If she paused, three doors would unlatch and the men—they each took a limb—can you see her struggle?

Her body most frequently surfaced in Queens.

One night, walking a friend's dog, I hinged a corner and faced a Russian: wide-boned, cropped hair, gold chain. In the streetlight's tangerine glaze, two more looked exactly like him. One wore a burgundy pleather jacket. A sedan idled at the curb, the driver's cigarette a red pinprick beneath the sunshade. Rust acne inflamed a skin of blue paint (did someone detail the hood's corrosion with *cornflower acrylic*?) No license plate.

I apprehended all of this in the time it took for the lucky screw I carried in my palm to ping on the sidewalk and bounce out of view.

"My friends, we need a light," the man said.

Two men cut in front of the sedan and the dog barked. The men recoiled. The man with the cigarette spit and said, "It's a fucking dog, you pussies!"

I sprinted past them—ten blocks—dog at my ankle, leash seared into the flesh of my hand. The welt curved like a lifeline.

2.9

My fear of abduction, of erasure, seeped into my language. I developed a fascination with the homophone's semantic peril, the homophone's spoken risk.

If the listener isn't really listening, at least one meaning hazards erasure; if the listener doesn't agree to recognize the homophone; if the listener doesn't fully invest in the interconnectedness of sound and space and meaning.

For example: *parish* and *perish*.

Through poetry, I learned that the reach of a steeple bell once defined a church's parish.

Where the sound perished, so did the word.

3.1

I have no recollection of the photos and messages that perished in the MySpace exodus, but I do recall the beige sensation of waiting for the upload status bar. The initial 50% of the upload would execute instantaneously; then, gradually, the increments: 55%; 66%, 72%; 87%; 91% (is there a mathematical expression for the MySpace upload percentage series?) before the bar would freeze; my black arrow hovering over *Update*, 98% stuck like a rusted hatch.

Lacking the proper editing software, my uncompressed videos timed out after twelve hours of uploading to YouTube. I wanted to smash my laptop.

Success in the Aughts aspired to hyper-completeness. Jeff Koons's "Balloon Dog," its candy-colored stainless steel iterations, delivered their cohesive shells. They reminded me of my roommate's cluster of blueberry, strawberry, tangerine, grape, and lime iMac G3 carcasses.

I wanted the "Balloon Dog" sculptures to be as compact as Skittles, as dense as Starbursts, as hard as Jolly Ranchers, but the sculptures' centers were empty. They were bubbles of air. I experienced a similar disenchantment the first time I bit into a gold-wrapped chocolate Easter bunny and discovered the treat wasn't solid.

My roommate promised he'd renovate the iMacs into aquariums and terrariums.

An empty center is a dystopian concept.

An empty center is a fragment.

3.2

In the Aughts, the ashes of Cormac McCarthy's *Road* cloak the Earth, destruction and carnage more atmosphere than event. Even cannibals suffer: cosmophages, they are all-mouth. The unspecific, ash-blurred geography of the dystopic globe implies that there is nowhere specific to run to: Our hero darts out of the frame, into an unnamed wood. This is no Edenic return. Our hero takes up refuge on the outskirts of the linear path to nowhere: an abandoned basement, a capsized ship, returning again to the road. The liminal property, the hero subsumed by process skirts its periphery, eternally returning to the road. Dystopia is nihilistic: Odysseus denied the circular route; the superhero denied the nemesis; the romantic denied even the idea of a girl; the ship denied the home port; the return itself betrayed: the homeland obsolete, homecoming a relic, and with it, the null set of redemption, resurrection, leaving only an impulse forward into the botched, the failure, the fracture, the fragment, the anecdote.

I won't pretend to be a cosmology.

I won't pretend to be an individual with an identity.

I sit on a park bench and scroll through the news.

3.3

When the bubble bursts, an acquaintance suggests I develop passive income. I Google "dividend stocks" and immerse myself in an investment clickhole. An SEO listicle boldly claims that Albert Einstein called compound dividends "the eighth wonder of the world."

This information is unverifiable.

According to Snopes.com, multiple versions of the urban legend persist. Einstein might have called compound interest "the most powerful force in the universe." He might also have called it "the greatest invention in human history."

Neologisms of the Aughts: *factoid, truthiness.*

By remembering incorrectly, we free ourselves of the past.

3.4

Pattern recognition was perfectly adequate.

The logic of the decade was the logic of a dream.

3.5

I was working as a barista in a rapidly-gentrifying neighborhood in Brooklyn when a regular struck up a conversation. He wanted to know what I did, not *what I did for money.* I told him I broke into abandoned buildings.

I told him about the Greenpoint Terminal Market, how my coworkers and I had shimmied up a waterfall of polyester clothing, cracked pipes, and molded insulation smeared with pigeon shit—a slew of debris almost thirty feet high— and how we slid down the fabric hills at the center of the warehouse, sledding on coats like cartoon penguins. I told him we'd scaled a wall using only the split lips of bricks and steel hooks to hoist us; how we'd climbed the elevator shaft up to the third floor; and how, when we reached the roof, we lay on the brick ledge overlooking the aluminum crinkle of the East River and let the sun bake our limbs as pigeon shit dried into chalk on our clothes.

"You privileged snot," the customer said. "You make a playground out of an eyesore. It's condescending. It's ruin porn."

Sir, I could argue for and against porn, for and against playgrounds and ruins.

Disillusioned by the accessible, I wanted what was forbidden; intact, I wanted what was beyond repair; like a man in a remote barracks pilots a drone across the planet, I wanted to tap the significance that dwelled in concentric circles of trespass around a notorious target. I wanted to drill my way into the center of something in a world of steadily increasing surfaces. I wanted the glass walls that keep me separate from you to become as permeable as air.

3.6

Q: Tell me a little something about pictures. Your pornographic pictures.

A: I developed one roll of film per week, kept the photographs in envelopes stacked in a cardboard box. When I subleased my room, I stored the box at my mother's house. I placed it next to my desk in my old bedroom. When I returned two months later, the box was gone.

Q: This is how you lost your photographs of the Greenpoint Terminal Market.

A: The aughts were years of lost things.

Q: And the building itself, it was a pornography?

A: The rooms were as large as basketball courts. They were filled with polyester clothing. The bundles were large as shipping containers, strapped in canvas and banded with rebar. In some rooms, where the ceiling leaked, the clothes were so frail that they dissolved when you touched them. On one side of the building, their damp weight caused the floorboards to collapse. There was one room in particular where you could balance on a beam and gaze down into the wreckage. Ailanthus sprouted

from the walls. You could shred the fabric with your fingers. The way we break hearts
just by looking. The way we save lives by listening.

    A: By cooking. I crushed vanilla beans into a sweet, malleable essence.

    A: I deboned myself.

    A: My favorite color of frosting.

3·7

On an extinct forum cached on the website of a gasket manufacturing company, I find my horror movie. Obsessed with quarry diving, I'm Google-searching the exact distance a body can leap into water without a fatal impact. On the messageboard, a man describes a game he played as a child in the abandoned marble quarries of Vermont: a game called "Al Capone's Vaults."

I ask S what she thinks of my idea: a movie based on "Al Capone's Vaults."

"No magic in it," S says. S. is obsessed with magic: David Copperfield, Harry Potter.

I step up my pitch with a speculative premise: Deep underwater, near the bottom of the quarry, there is a singularity. You cannonball into the water. The deeper you swim, the faster time accelerates. By the time you've unfurled your legs and kicked, gasping, to the surface, years have passed. You're too arthritic to tread water, too frail to grasp the rope hitched to the ledge.

"Does anyone die?" S asks. Yes, almost everyone.

Until they catch on to what's happening. Then the horror becomes *how to dive and surface and live as a ten-year-old trapped in a ninety-year-old body.*

S objects. "Too much death and dying. Why are you so obsessed with darkness?"

"Abjection becomes splendor," says Deleuze. "The horror of life creates a very pure and very intense life."

I suppose I'm drawn to abjection and horror because an abject life, a life that survives its horror, is a life charged with intensity.

3.8

The building survived because it was built to survive.
It was built before planned obsolescence.
It was built before materiality's future was a studied thing.
It was built before decay was academic.
It was built before decay was an aesthetic.
It was built before one could type:
"Ruin is a Romantic construct, but Modernism loaned us decay."
It was built before blister packs
and stampedes on Black Friday.
It was built before layoffs
and H1-B outsourcing.
It was built before logos on black glass windows.
It was built before helipads and networked security.
It was built before data
and data entry. It was built before data
resembled fact.
It was built in the corporation's earliest century.
It was built before legal corporate personhood. It was built

before corporations had personalities.
Before a corporation would abandon its buildings.
Like a deadbeat dad walks out on his family.
Like a rocket disengages spent fuel cells
to preserve its upward trajectory.
O pencil and pencil eraser.
O Wite-Out and ballpoint pen.
O Adam Smith and Wealth of Nations.
Sometimes it feels our personal property
is the only right we have.
And even then.

3.9

By the end of the Aughts, I'd ditched the Q & A.

4.1

Like a quarry jumper, I inspect my rope; its narrative tethers me to my decade. The ends of my rope are equally as important as the length in the middle. I can't discuss the Aughts without discussing the tail of the 90s and the after-Aughts' early fringe. My rope is fractal geometry and Y2K and *A Million Little Pieces* and the World Wide Web. My rope is quantitative easing and Occupy Wall Street and a kite's pure surface and adjunct shame. My rope is porous, unstable, variable. At best, my rope is Zeno's arrow. At its worst, it's the sum of my subtractions.

4.2

In the 90s, my lyrics included: flicked cigarettes, steel darts, traffic flares, jealous cathedrals, late fame, ultraviolet eyes, neon lights, red moons, sweet powder, glossy magazines, pills for ills, concrete vines, neon lights, a girl with no face.

In the Aughts: cats, ghosts, sweaters, claws, dirt, work, the highway, the road, the interstate, hail, hay, halos, fields, wolves, whales, lambs, loons, ice, oaks, glass, matchsticks, temples, aspens, tongues, chapels, mountain lions, lightning, pines, wires, soil, sun, bells, ravens, egrets, muscles, sand, salt flats, glands, badlands, brands, myrtle, bees, bears, scarabs, squirrels, thorns, pearls, lions, steel, lead, gloves, comfort, summer, holes, fire, echoes, hum, parents, yellow eyes, copper, dust, fur, sage grass, prairies, lockets, promises, wicker, hands, headlights, stars, cities, boulders, green grass, concrete, cormorants, ocean, breakers, minerals, unions, horizons, rakes, fathers, coats, wallets, records, youth, crows, switch motels, cellular towers, foil, butter-colored grass, fools, you, worries, cypresses, moss, razors, souls, tigers, icicles, bands, edges of towns, helicopters, prisms (though I might have sang *prisons*), swamps, black water, thunder, difference, branches, leaves, owls, sleep, dreams, bats, mice, crickets, hours, power, the street.

In the 90s, modified nouns.
In the Aughts, adjectives decommissioned.

In the 90s, the city.
In the Aughts, thoroughfares and switch motels. Prairies and salt flats and swamps.

In the 90s, potencies that flare and go out.
In the Aughts, a pastoral residue.

4.3

"[The painter] does not paint
in order to reproduce . . .

he paints on images
that are already there." —Deleuze

In no decade have I ever relinquished the image.

An image relates to other images.

Facebook made these connections visible.

And valuable.

4.4

The Aughts witnessed the valuation of conection: fashions of the present, tethered to tropes past. The Aughts witnessed the beginning of the 90s revival. 80s, 70s, 60s, 50s fetishism was present, too. I listened to the warm fuzz-ed out hits of The Strokes, The Black Keys, Vivian Girls. Joanna Newsom opened for Devendra Banhart at Bowery Ballroom and I went home and listened to Karen Dalton, Vashti Bunyan, and Tyrannosaurus Rex. Antony and The Johnsons were awarded the Mercury Prize and I put on Nina Simone's "Wild is the Wind." My roommate started a DIY business selling hand-sewn cherry-print aprons. I wanted to bastardize William Carlos Williams: *No present but in past.* I wanted to import myself into the canon, the *rolling blackouts of retro fashions.* I went thrift shopping. Some fashions were vintage; some fashions were artifacts. Some fashions were trash. Some records were collectors' items; some records shattered in dumpsters. The past wasn't evenly distributed.

The future isn't evenly distributed, either. Who do you need to be to be remembered?

4.5

The past is plausible, but in flux. The past is an unreliable narrator. When I learned that Yves Klein's "Leap into the Void" was a doctored image, I understood that all acts of freedom and abandon have been carefully cultivated since 1960. Of course, I already lived the ethos: Livejournal taught me *To Be Continued*. Blogspot taught me to draft and revise. I weeded my Flickr like an English garden.

If you expect to find a hero in the Aughts, good luck. A hero needs a beginning, a discrete origin, a locus of suffering, and we have evolved to cite multiple sources, try out various plotlines, annihilate all outwards signs of suffering. A hero needs an absolute and we hedge at action. Will you click on my petition? Will you thumbs-up my opinion? A hero is totalitarian, a time-honored symbol of the whole, first in its potency, then in its triumph, and finally, in its cruelty. How can we be cruel? Here is a kitten.

A hero's end is his origin. He can't go back, but he must go back. He can reverse time by spinning Earth on its axis. If you think about it, Superman would be a very scary man.

We can't go back, but we must go back.

#TBT, a miniskirt. #TBT, a headband.

4.6

Somewhere in the middle of the decade, American culture reached peak-superhero. Great American Novelists set down their suburban realism to investigate the superhero psyche: What would it be like to have *power*?

The novels weren't concerned with truth of the superhero lifestyle (of which there is none: superheroes don't exist), but whether or not the story *worked*. Whether or not the story was loyal to its own internal logic. Whether or not the superhero's struggle translated as *sincere*. The drive of psychological superhero fiction is to investigate the human burdens of power; to expose the strain of power's responsibility; to make visible the *real man* behind the stupendous acts, the bold drag, the boasts and brags.

Transparency was an emergent feature: Wikileaks distributed documents from Guantánamo in the name of transparency. Investigators demanded transparency regarding journalists' CIA sources, the same transparency the NSA commanded from American citizens. The transparency of logged keychain searches, character strings, the click-prints we dribble as we tap, link, and share; the transparency of networked medical records, phone bills, credit card statements, Netflix and YouTube streams; the transparency of TSA x-rays, pat-downs, rub-downs, and strip-searches; the transparency of tell-all confessionals and *Who Wore It Best?* and nanny cams and sex tapes and vapor suspension nanotechnology and strip mall radiology; the transparency of unencrypted mobile banking data; the transparency of evidence.

Never forget: When we identify with the superhero, we empathize with power.

A man with x-ray vision can disrobe you without your consent.

4·7

Confession: I watched *The Incredibles* three times, and only once on an airplane. The man I mistakenly loved and I devoured expert online testimony regarding the hypothetical mechanics of x-ray vision glasses, invisibility fabric, the Death Star's trash compactor, syntactical errors in Klingon insults, the physics of faster-than-light (FTL) propulsion systems, also known as Warp Drive.

Fiction's hand was stuck in nonfiction's cookie jar, and vice versa.

Fact was an anachronism. Data was the new black.

There was a wait list to supercompute the distant transmissions of starbursts; a wait list to crunch the hypotheses of tenured and adjunct number theorists; a wait list for the large hadron collider. There was a wait list for the best colorist at the hair salon at the end of the block; an endless supply of stylists; an endless supply of color.

4.8

First there is the data, then there is the data about the data.

Data multiplies like mayflies, like questions from questions.

Every date becomes suddenly aware of every other date in the calendar.

Behind every data set, a secret minnow.

Rocks in a stream.

Not the data but our relation to it. Not the fallout but the calibration of our instruments. There is no organizing principle to a person or a century; the wallpaper rearranges its parrots; the streaming sensation is how we perceive the rate of the change. The *mystical nature of the commodity* over-ripens on outer-borough billboards, in placard windows and cubicle hallways.

The late-Aughts' trickle-down emergencies: new human emotions that haven't yet been named; malignant cancers unfurling hourly; the disappearance of a hazmat sign from a defunct nursery; the urge to quit my job and cross the country; an assortative adoration for an unknown equal I can't locate; soft streetlight humidity, ailanthus boughs in the open window in lieu of A/C.

4.9

I wake in the dark at the lip of the canyon. When light breaks on the desert pines, I rise for one last stroll down the incline. That's when I see the ram. He looks at me with a walnut eye. He shows me his horns. They are heavier than all of his bones.

In El Paso, the border police are confused by my houseplants. I can't abandon my houseplants. As a kid, I had a rubber plant named Julio who grew so tall he scraped the ceiling. When Julio turned brown, I couldn't eat. Pothos, Ficus, Bleeding Hearts. Hens and Chicks and English Ivy. I race across the country with a car full of leaves.

Past midnight in the central lowlands, I hallucinate a blizzard. So dizzy, I almost vomit. The car skids into the byway and I stagger out onto dirt. Inhale the hot dust in the headlights. The sky above agape with stars. The hood of my car isn't frozen. It's encrusted with the bodies of thousands of moths.

That's the way I wrote in the Aughts: I wrote scenes for an audience of one. I wrote as though I were sending him postcards. As though I were speeding towards him. I wrote as though there were a trajectory. It didn't mean that I knew him. He was a song I might've written late night as I drifted off. How did he go. Where was I driving. I wanted to live out the rest of the record.

In San Antonio, I crash on the couch of a friend from the internet. She takes me to the dive bar where Nirvana played their first show in Texas. We drink Lone Star, cruise to the Alamo even though it's closed. I use my disposable camera to photograph her friend who's recently split her tongue like a lizard. The lizard tongue is blue. She's sipping a blue raspberry Slurpee.

When I arrive in Atlanta, I drive in circles, so many circles it's almost holy.

My friend from college lends me his parking space in Chapel Hill. He drives me to Duke Gardens where we duck beneath foliage to find more foliage in the humidity. We lay for a while at the lip of a black lily pond. Any man with a microphone can tell you where to find what you'd thought you'd wanted. A friend will allow you to find nothing at all.

There's a field we drive to at three in the morning, bundles of blankets in our arms. Side by side, under the blankets, we lie in the frost and watch the meteors. One meteor is green as lichen. I throw my hand in the air and spread my fingers. That's how long the tail is. A meteor the size of my hand.

5.1

In the Aughts, tragedy unfurled its loss in sharp, unvaried patterns.

Violent language spiked up from ashes and floods.

Hate speech neologisms (~~towelhead~~, ~~sandnigger~~) were performative utterances that instantly and utterly debased both victim and perpetrator.

I now pronounce you shame and shame.

5.2

"So many of the people in the arena here, you know, were underprivileged anyway, so this is working very well for them," chirped Barbara Bush in a televised interview following a tour of the Astrodome in the aftermath of Hurricane Katrina.

To suggest that Barbara Bush's statement lacks empathy is an understatement, but at least she refers to people as *people*, at least she is willing to share her proximity ("here").

(How generous.)

A decade later, also in a televised interview, police officer Darren Wilson (white, armed, adult) said, of shooting Michael Brown (black, unarmed, child): "It won't haunt me. It will just be something that happened."

Michael Brown, "It."

"It will be just . . ."

"It will be . . . happened."

As though the future were already in the past, as though he were pulling out in front of it, cutting the future off in tense. His commentary, a traffic infraction.

5.3

A Twitter handle named TRAIN RESPECTOR tweets:

What's the deal with airplane food?
1. It's usually called jet fuel
2. It doesn't burn hot enough to melt steel beams

A symbolic return to the past often marks an uncertainty in the present.

"We become what we behold," writes Marshall McLuhan. By the time I arrive in the city, it's been dark for the length of a work day. I can park anywhere—there are no signs.

Steel beams like blue taffy. Symmetrical rectilinear structures enclosed around symmetrical rectilinear structures rendered amorphous, discontinuous, polyphonic, as roots range, advance by cellular intuition even when crushed, impacted, or transplanted, they return to biology's sensitivity. A renunciation of logic's sequential argument captured and delivered by logic's sequential frame.

"We shape our tools, and thereafter our tools shape us." One year later: *sodium streetlights' orange glaze transmogrified the white spears of titanium kliegs.*

Sodium light, a soft light, diffuses. Titanium lights are hard, discrete; they are on a structure, across a structure. On a humid night, a titanium spotlight's column sprouts, Ionic, from the mist as though imported from the Parthenon.

5.4

In her essay "Pain Tours," Leslie Jamison writes of Edmund Burke's "negative pain," a delight that emerges when fear and safety are experienced simultaneously. Television viewers experience "negative pain" while watching cop shows, action and horror flicks, the local evening news. Television is the portal that draws the menace close while keeping the risk safely at bay.

Our computers are portals, silver lozenges of light. They are machine; they do as we design them to do. Their sterile ergonomics buffer us from the actual peril that bubbles beyond the representations of pain smoothly delivered by the invisible pulse of buried fiber-optic cable. Intimations of pain ripple like a tainted aquifer. Our ability to depress our power buttons and shut the whole thing down reinforces the illusion that we man the surveillance rooms of our experience.

In the Aughts we are awed, neither by the forces of nature, nor by the depths and heights of human endeavor, but by the fact that humans, too, are the horror of nature. That our detachment from our carnage is another form of violence.

5.5

Our songbirds evolved to migrate
  nocturnally, when predators
  retire and winds die, but now,
  in the sky above the Tribute
  in Light, whorl in the white floodlit
  condensation. Smog, particle
  suspension, whatever the news
  calls the stale fractal void, birds flit
  between its bright spokes and the
  dark site, impossible to track
  any one bird for any length
  of time as they coil, blind and
  wailing in the bold false dawn that
  lured them inside the fingerprint.

5.6

I felt the spiral—was it History? I didn't feel the need to be linear in the way I portrayed my life onscreen. I didn't feel beholden to a career path. I experienced the legacy of my elders and of the American government as a series of distinct betrayals: taxes, joblessness, medical costs, Boomer disdain followed by the disdain of Gen X, the new gatekeepers who had suddenly realized that what they wanted, aside from flex time, authenticity, and the right to publicly sulk, was what their predecessors wanted: income, stability, family, homeownership, creative legacy. Maslow's hierarchy of needs came as a wide-paneled stepladder for those with privilege, but not for the majority of Millennials. 9/11 united Americans, for a brief duration. The electoral college failed the individuals who voted in the popular election. I joined 500,000 bodies in the bone-cold march against the Iraq War in February of 2003. Riot police in Stormtrooper costumes lined the roofs of federal buildings and the grassy knolls of the National Mall. The numbers reported in the news hardly reflected our masses. Troops were deployed despite us. Narratives of vengeance, expansion, and greed masqueraded as narratives of solidarity, pride, and charity. Masqueraded as origin myths.

Operation Active Endeavour, Operation Enduring Freedom, Operation Iraqi Freedom, Operation New Dawn.

The truthy inconsistencies: there were no WMDs; jet fuel can't melt steel beams.

As a young girl, I knew the phrase "a shot heard around the world" before I could tell you what the world was.

The things Americans are most proud of originate in a bang.

5·7

In the Aughts, I knew about the Big Bang, but I had no sense of a discrete origin or an original unity. I didn't believe in a patronymic god. Despite my eagerness to side with the heroes of science, I was reluctant to believe the world ballooned from a single violent burst. I'd read Galtung; I knew how the cosmogony and cosmology of a civilization act as a socio-cultural code, a kind of DNA that determines how a culture will perceive reality and that carries instructions for what they will do with it.

In the Aughts, I burned with a mad desire to originate, to harbor a source of authenticity, to become myself an authentic burst. I recorded songs to a Tascam 4-track; I hand-stitched cases for burned CDs. When my art failed me, when my career path crashed and scattered, instead of resorting to violence, I subsumed myself in the slow fizzle, the diffuse dissolve of remnants. Vintage sequins twinkled in the back of my closet. My drawers were a foam of little originals. My style was the style of space scrap.

5.8

I changed scraps when I changed my username. My early-Aughts logins: *fashionableboar, jonbonjovee, michelmustoo.* After a while of wisecracking under an alias, I wanted to connect. I registered "jasminedreame."

In the beginning of the Aughts, people didn't believe *Jasmine Dreame* was my given name. The reviews editor for a prominent literary magazine made fun of my name on his blog: "Unless she was born while her parents partied at Woodstock,

I'd bet she made that middle name up," he blogged. "Does having such a nifty nom-de-plume help an author get published?" No, asshole. It doesn't.

I asked my Livejournal followers if I should adopt the semi-pseudonym "J. D. Wagner." A. M. Homes and C. D. Wright had used initials to successfully constrain the excesses of their gender. *Jasmine Dreame Wagner* was how I looked on the outside, but *J. D. Wagner* more closely aligned with my ambition. When my followers' votes aligned in the semi-pseudonym's favor, my innards folded like a dented can of fruit. Only one person rallied for my name. "Fuck that noise," wrote an old love. "There is only one Jasmine Dreame Wagner."

I decided I would create and maintain one consistent vessel for the promulgation of my personality. That vessel would have a consistent username; its events would run parallel to the events of my IRL identity. I would use my given name.

Then I realized there is no IRL.

The internet, and what happens on the internet, is as real as the keyboard in front of me.

5.9

George W. Bush serenaded us from an airplane. Eminem released a movie. I downloaded "Lose Yourself" (mp3, free). I saw Damian Hirst's "The Impossibility of Death in the Mind of Someone Living," the shark suspended in formaldehyde, at The Metropolitan Museum of Art. I tapped on the glass. The docent didn't notice. (Neither did the shark.) I saw Edward Burtynsky's Brooklyn Museum retrospective, his C-prints of shipbreaking in Bangladesh, uranium tailings, copper and marble and mineral mines, heaps of discarded circuit boards, tires, and wires. Chris Ofili used scat to paint. Dash Snow jerked off into a pile of tabloids. (It's referred to as "works on paper" and "collage" by the curator at the Whitney.)

The old art was rotten with materials.

Outside the museum, Giuliani cleaned up New York City. I rode the subway from Times Square to Brooklyn, strolled home unaccompanied and mostly unaddressed. The last time I was assaulted on the subway was at rush hour at the end of the 90s. The car was packed. I was seated, reading Mary Gaitskill's *Because They Wanted To,* when a man opened his camel hair coat and tried to shove his erect penis into my mouth. Immersed in Gaitskill, I didn't at first recognize the penis so I batted it away with my book. I only knew it was a cock when I registered a yeasty smell. I exited swiftly at the next stop.

This never would have happened after 9/11. After 9/11, I wouldn't have frozen. I would have mauled him. Or he wouldn't have been there. After 9/11, he would have been a cop.

Cops manned the subway cars in quads and pairs. *Navy blue petals on a black bough.* Late night in the Aughts, I watched two cops sleep standing up. They swayed with the engine.

6.1

In the Aughts, I quoted Rilke in a zine I wrote called *Songs About Ghosts.* "Try to love the questions themselves, like locked rooms, or books written in a foreign language," Rilke offers. "Do not now look for the answers. They cannot now be given to you, because you would not be able to live them."

The sun slips behind the strand of oaks, disclosing the orange bruise of the city behind the treetops. On the television, a newsflash: an "active shooter situation."

How many times does Rilke use the word *now*.

6.2

From Wikipedia:

The Columbine High School massacre was a school shooting that occurred on April 20, 1999.

The Sandy Hook Elementary School shooting occurred on December 14, 2012.

Columbine is referred to as a "massacre [that] was a school shooting."

Newtown is referred to as a "shooting."

The last time the word "massacre" is used in the Wikipedia database of school shootings is April 16, 2007: Virginia Tech.

Adjectives decommissioned. Sentences whittled down.

In the Aughts, the opposite of cause is not effect.

The opposite of cause is the cause's reverberation.

6.3

—writes Gaston Bachelard, paraphrasing Eugène Minkowski. Bachelard is speaking of a poetic image's "sonority," the way in which a poet's images are transmitted: Poetic images have no cause, they resonate free of causality, like a water droplet's ripple. In poetry, there is no droplet, only the ripple.

When Bachelard implies that an image doesn't have a cause, he means that a poetic image isn't a product of logic.

Bachelard's poetic image doesn't originate from an actual edge (like a knife), doesn't stem from the idea of an edge (like the idea of a knife). It must only embody the ethos of the edge. It must emit a frequency that cuts.

> *My Life had stood – a Loaded Gun –*   *(Dickinson)*

> *Among the red guns In the hearts of soldiers*   *(Sandburg)*

6.4

My watch is broken. I don't know why
I expect a gatekeeper
of time to be permanent. I suppose

I believe in an heirloom mythos.

The way things are; the way the world is.

I have never carved an altar,

I don't burn incense

but I have squinted backwards over my shoulder.

I have dug out my unkempt nails.

Some shootings reverberate through the media.

I am helpless as a crumpled ear.

What dying has not felt noteworthy?

The moon beeps: busy, busy, busy. Outside,

a car deflates like a bloodless lung.

Snow

arrives for Peter Lanza. RAID

Kills Bugs Dead.

And drives him to Canada.

My inbox is a slaughterhouse.

Everything advertised is a torso.

A car arrives.

I try to be kind to myself but I am not my master.

God is the Father Jesus The Father The Almighty The Holy Ghost.

A car. Remember: The sonnet

is not natural but artificial, not wild and innate

but tamed. Some shootings are brownouts.

Cornrows, baby birds.

Kill.com Kill.org Kill.net Kill.gov Kill.co.uk

Remember: The ease

with which you configure your profile,

the gerund, indicates class. An unconscious inhibition

affects everything you say or do. Or just:

Do. Because speech is an act.

Granny and son want a taxidermy boy for their mantelpiece.

I drive past the prayer shawls, Bibles, teddy bears, "My First Christmas in Heaven,"
crosses, crystals, salted caramels.

A WHITE BOY

A car for Peter
Lanza. My willingness to splay my guts
online indicates both aspirational tendencies
and downward mobility. I fantasize
about shooting a rifle
into the belly
of an angel food cake, rip
a magazine to shreds
and begin again, with clover. Or an XJ (X350).
A car.
The ocean is not at fault
for the bloat of a beautiful body.
It is a black hole.
Fake plastic trees in a ring around it.
Crickets', tree frogs' recorded chirps.
I remember the first time
I saw a $1,000 bill.
It looked like it had washed up
in a flash flood of early men. *WHERE WAS THE MOTHER?*
It trapped my madness for the world
in material witness.
"No Bugs, No Hassles"
"Honor God in All We Do"
-TERMINIX

It was democratic green.
PSYCHO KILLER
My early watercolors demonstrated
a keen instinct for totalitarian orange.
I had no words
for millennia, chrome, taupe, spatter-pattern, demiurge.
But I knew the cheese puff's empty volume
and the pleasure I derived from crushing one.

6.5

By the end of the Aughts, I stop writing songs and start writing fragments.
The snow goes viral online. The sky blazes over the economic doldrums. What
could be a shutdown is reworded. The archive becomes apparent as we become
proficient in shaming it. Sand dunes shif, bidding to be sculpted into something
permanent.

> *Here is a revolver*

> *It has an amazing language all its own*   *(Sandberg)*

6.6

The building had no fixed meaning.
> *To some it was redlined.*
> *To some it was a gray lacuna on a map.*
> *To some it was connected to actionable airspace.*

To some it was a set.

To some it was a hyperbolic ideal, a new arcadia, an apocalyptic vision.

To some it was a portal to a future past.

To some, its participation in the visual field offered
the brotherhood of failure
to the sisterhood of silence.

To some it was a grapefruit injected with vodka.

To some it was a rape kit.

To some it was time's bankruptcy, a bubble burst, insolvency.

To some it was a queer read of unstable identity:

It inhabited both
the role of spectator (it scrutinized the trespasser's nakedness)
and performer (it was as costumed as we were).

6.7

In the Aughts, a building's decay was indicative of its neighborhood's location on the periphery of the middle class. It contained implicit instructions for encroaching. For causing a ruckus. For staying in the game far beyond its limits.

The building was both aspirational and anarchic. It promised that time would undo the structures that outspent themselves.

Rappelling down the warehouse wall, a gel capsule: a moment, safe, but close to dissolving in the acid rain.

Rappelling was a costless leisure, but *what leisure is there, amid atrocity, that does not feel like an extension of that horror?* (Agamben)

6.8

When I photographed the building with my disposable camera, I didn't yet know that a photograph of a ruin multiplies the ruin's surfaces. I didn't yet know that by surfaces I meant orifices. Ruins and images of ruins remind us that our bodies, our skin, our bones, are porous, vulnerable, exposed.

I didn't yet know how abstraction can be both freedom and funeral for a figure. How a building's declension to abstraction connotes a plea for a feral sincerity; how forms, when appropriated, are strip-mined of meaning; how I would trawl the language of immaterial structures, immaterial processes, the language of language, in search of philosophy.

In search of poetry.

6.9

At the beginning of the Aughts, I wanted to subsume myself within the ruin's field. I wanted to burrow my way into its center. By the end of the decade, I wanted to stand at the edge of the field, observe the field and my observing it.

Maturity? Or a reaction to a decade's worth of surveillance?

I listened to Damian Jurado's "Like Titanic" over and over again.

7.1

In the Aughts, coffee shop soundtracks were wet with reverb. I wondered if the music would sound so deep, so profound, if the production weren't soaked.

Reverb introduces space between the performer and the listener. It transports the performer from her studio to front of a concert hall. It imparts a distance and a grandeur that isn't necessarily true to the performance. It implies that the music is popular enough to be performed in an ampitheater. Reverb recasts the bedroom performer as an idol.

Reverb reveals the desire not to be a musician, but to be an influence.

7.2

Reverb forestalls critical distance. It separates the listener from the performer. The greater the distance between a listener and a performer, the less the listener participates in the performance. In the widening gap, the listener becomes a critic.

7.3

Reverb glosses over errors. Reverb is a finishing glaze. It is the *maximum gloss enhancement* offered by an auto body shop.

7.4

Hall reverb coats the snare in a patina of nostalgia found in staged battles of historical reenactment.

Cathedral reverb on the guitar is a tenured poet's aubade for Christ's crucifixion.

Room reverb on the voice is Siri's personification of Mnemosyne.

Plate reverb on the flute is Pan soloing in a dumpster.

7.5

The cacophony of lo-fi indie rock reverb evokes angst and structural violence. It is the sound of gentrification, the sound of a place becoming economically out of reach for those who caused it to become economically out of reach, the sound of that shame, a humiliated sound. It's the sound of *if only*. It's the sound of *why me*. It's the sound of *an era whose dream forgot me*.

It's also the sound of *why not me*.

It's also the sound of *not me*.

7.6

In the Aughts, the reverb of gentrified Brooklyn became more a capitalistic veneration than an artistic device. Despite the futuristic utopian collectivity of downloads, streams, and torrents, music profits took a nosedive. Revivalism was born again as a brand story that evoked a time when artists and executives could earn fortunes or at least make an upper-middle class living by harnessing and distributing sound. Reverb signified a shift in consumer alliance with the *now* to the *then*.

The past surged in popularity. Surf-rock was everywhere, so much that the roar of water coalesced in a new conformity. In folk, indie, rock, and pop, the vocal and the snare swam in distant waters. In the "authentic" pools of DIY, a movement that banked on authenticity, the use of reverb ran deepest. First it was a sonic costume, then a uniform.

Dominant trends emerged from gentrified neighborhoods of wealthy cities. Blogs and mainstream press required new music to be promoted through boutique public relations outfits if the tunes were to be reviewed as legitimate. Brand managers and web analytics filled the holes in *Artist & Repertoire*. Sound was consumed only after its accompanying image passed muster, weather-filter worn and sun-filter faded. Reverb taught its audience to desire: an address in the past, an intermediate agent, visibility and consistency through repetition. Scarcity. (When is a day more valued: when you are living it—or when it has been extinguished?)

Listen:

Before the Aughts, Converse and Mountain Dew were products. During the Aughts, Converse and Mountain Dew were brands.

In the Aughts, Converse and Mountain Dew became curators. Mountain Dew incorporated Green Label Sound. Converse opened a chain of recording studios for sponsored bands: Converse Rubber Tracks.

Movies used to feature *product placement*. Products would pay a fee to enter into a fictional narrative. In the Aughts, products hired humans to play roles in the product's narrative. In the Aughts, products have *human placement*.

I would say, the product's *timeline*. But *timeline* suggests Facebook.

I mean, History.

History: Since the Supreme Court's end-of-the-Aughts ruling in Citizens United, Converse and Mountain Dew have held the same rights as people.

In order to secure a voice equal to those of corporations, in order to become larger than life, people become brands. Qualities of successful brands, such as media visibility, message consistency, and financial solvency become measures of human achievement.

Visibility, consistency, solvency, become moral imperatives.

7.8

The end of the Aughts culminated in the birth of Lana Del Rey, Inc., a reverbed cyborg of conservative values and post-war nostalgia packaged in trickle-down economics and third-wave feminism.

Lana Del Rey is the late-Aughts' most successfully contrived media scarab, entombing Lana Turner's wardrobe, Brigitte Bardot's bouffant, Marilyn Monroe's suicidal ideation, the background radiation of the entertainment and military industrial complexes, in Elizabeth Grant's ambitious amber.

Lana Del Rey's *daddy* is a dot com millionaire. This fact is relevant and irrelevant. It is part of her brand story, a part that is officially erased and reported unofficially. Two press campaigns: the tender underbelly and the surface.

Celebrity in the Aughts requires equal parts erasure and exposure. What is exposed is denied or erased; what is erased or denied is exposed.

Lana Del Rey often invokes Walt Whitman, whose use of anaphora and extended praise evokes the *Song of Solomon*.

Lana Del Rey sings: "It's you, it's you, it's all for you. Everything I do."

"Everything I do, I do it for you," sang Bryan Adams in 1991.

Lana Del Rey is a master of echolalia, as she ought to be, as a product of the Aughts.

7.9

If you want to hear the unadulterated, you'll have to shed all expectations of melody and structure (and money) and to listen to noise.

8.1

In the Aughts, I lived in New York, California, Montana, and Connecticut. I traveled to Zurich, Beirut, Baalbek, Douma, Tyre, Cyprus, London, Brighton, Bournemouth, Edinburgh, Inverness, The Isle of Skye, Montreal, Toronto, Halifax, Cape Breton, Prince Edward Island, Helsinki, Tallinn, Paldiski, Haapsalu, Gothenburg, Oslo, Bergen, Tromso, Trondheim, The Lofoten Islands, Rome, Florence, Naples, Moscow, St. Petersburg, Nairobi, The Rift Valley, Cairo, Barcelona. I drove across the United States of America five times.

My movements, the longest poem I've written, is a lifelong durational sculpture documenting my love for the exit, the gaze back, the return, my hands in the dirt.

8.2

An origin story: I was alphabetizing the bookshelves at the coffee shop where I worked when I discovered William Wenthe's *Birds of Hoboken*. Wenthe described a recognizable world: I walked the East River—the smokestacks, their feverish reflections in the current—I tried to describe the feeling that the gulls and the ruined shore imparted in me, but I hadn't yet learned the words.

Yeats writes of the Minor Genius: ". . . he often plucks flowers by the wayside and ties them into knots and garlands."

Gaston Bachelard writes: "We are never real historians, but always near poets."

I was a graduate student when I first read G.C. Waldrep's poem, "The Batteries." Waldrep's description of the barges, how they "socket past" "like small planets," reminded me of the view from the Shore Road green space between Owl's Head Park and the Verrazano, where, during the winter after 9/11, I watched the barges' blue and red blocks ghost in and out of the Narrows as soldiers crested the ridge. "Trade," Waldrep writes, "is like war, only slower."

Presence and remoteness were one.

I think of Bachelard writing of immensity, how he explains that we are not "cast into the world," "we open the world," and how Wenthe laments: "It is too far / to call back the first time / the appearance of a bird above the river / opened a new world." The birds return.

Roethke writes: "I learn by going where I have to go."

It is through poetry that I learned how a threshold is the place where the individual becomes aware of their connection to the enormity of being. Between what's past and what's anticipated, the infinite present emerges.

8.3

An origin story: J and I meet in the morning at the Tallinn train station. We buy pastries in wax paper and wander the tented market that springs up daily along the tracks. J rifles through a vendor's used army gear: wool pants, wool jackets emblazoned with geometric patches. Aluminum gun tripods. There are shelves stocked with armies of rubber dolls; animals with plastic teardrop eyes and mushroom-stump legs; steel clips in tin pans; rusted cartoon carnation pins.

I know enough about Estonian history to recognize the carnations as cornflowers. The cornflower, a blue wildflower that grows in rye fields, is Estonia's national flower. The blue stripe that runs through the middle of the national flag is *cornflower blue*. Under Soviet occupation, cornflower decorations were banned from public spaces. The blue petals were painted over with red enamel; in vases, flowers' stems were fed red dye and renamed.

The symbol gained potency. Blue endured below the red bursts. Embroidered carnations connoted undisclosed sentiment. The gift of a bouquet hand-picked from the rye fields bloomed with meaning. Men wore cornflower stems in their buttonholes as a silent pledge.

I run my fingertips over the buttons. Collectibles are out of my budget; I have only enough cash for the train. I'm not sure if I should call them collectibles, if they are jewelry, adornment, if they are artifacts. If they are old enough to be imbued with History's dignity, or if I should call them memorabilia, souvenirs: little memorials, objects not to archive, but to thumb until the color rubs out.

J reaches up and plies a gas mask from an array of ventilation tubes, chemical goggles, sound-damping earmuffs, and other assorted military paraphernalia that dangle, bunched in clusters like grapes, from fishing nets nailed to the ceiling of the stall. He taps the masks with the fascination of an infant grasping for a mobile. The masks are for sale—to remember, or to use?

Once we're on the train, J unfolds the map. It's smaller than I'd imagined, the length of my forearm. We smooth it across our laps.

Landscape scrolls through the window's frame: gray and yellow homes, a backyard garden's plump loaves of snow, barbed wire's split ends, blanched tarpaulins. A byway of frozen mud puddles is replaced with ribbons of blue and red and pink graffiti. Where the graffiti frays: open land, a cubic palette of gray, raw umber, soft black hardened to titanium white, alcoves of spruce and pine, a stone home, smoke billowing from its chimney, ice-coated birches poking up from the ground like singed filaments of light bulbs.

For a moment, I forget how I relish privacy. I want to share this.

8.4

Burtynsky's mines:

An origin story: He desired
a discernable vortex,
one perfect circle of sunlight.

Did not witness the dove
as it keeled into the Anaconda pit in Butte;

did witness
the Anaconda pit in Butte.

The angles of the tracks
where the tracks led.

He desired the fact
of dirt, the stasis

of a still filled with grass
like the hair of a Doberman
combed back.

8.5

The barracks, whose outer walls and rafters recall the shells of desiccated beetles, spill into a residential microdistrict at the end of the train yard.

The easternmost district blocks appear to be occupied. Their yellow paint is badly oxidized; vertical cracks sprout between units, reinforced with the same tar that patches the potholes in the street. To the west, the units aren't so fortunate. In the midday shade, their green eggshell coatings are chipped, flaking in patches like eczema, revealing concrete and insulation. Windows are cracked or missing, with gaps like knocked-out teeth. Dead nettles wither along the sidewalks. In a planned community designed to promote equality, an uneven distribution of structural decay pocks the cultivated sterility.

In the vestibule of a green building, the dirt floor is littered with broken bottles, foils and wrappers, cartons and boxes. The walls are streaked with flared scars, burn marks from an aerosol can aimed over a lighter. Someone has tagged the far wall: a flutter of resistance. I think of the Sunset Park waterfront, the Greenpoint Terminal Market—the ailanthus a lush forest, shades of green layered on concrete's orange, purple, and yellow zigzags; slabs that read "OBSOLETE MACHINES" and "LOVE LIES / HERE" like tombstone engravings; "NECK FACE"; an octopus in a spacesuit like a communiqué from a future where, submerged in air, language has retracted into pictogram.

Graffiti, a language of pure economy, is utopian, a nonverbal reckoning of our oldest themes. The longing for a closed and sterile world can never be more than a longing. The promise of a homogenous world, a secure world, isn't a performative pact—it, too, is a tag, scribed with flair, impermanent.

8.6

An origin story: at ABC No Rio, a crust band screams about smashing surfaces. The merch guy has a VHS recorder and a point-and-shoot. He's documenting the concert for public access. He scrawls down the Geocities address where he documents his expeditions into closed subway stations. From my laptop, I watch him. As the Aughts progress, he branches out into boarded-up mental wards and institutions. I care about his progress, his snapshots of articulate fragments that evade effacement, the way he achieves liberation by looking for no one. During his attempt to ford the East River by canoe to access the Roosevelt Island Smallpox Hospital, the Coast Guard arrests him. The blog comes down.

8.7

On the white Baltic, the sun closes in on the horizon. A fishing vessel—the *Aries*—tips to one side, bolstered by ice blocks thick as the concrete slabs of Brutalist monuments. There isn't another craft in sight, only the sea, flat as a salt-encrusted parking lot. Limestone cliffs surge from the water in severe verticality: this is the Baltic Klint, a mass of sedimentary rock unhindered by wind, tectonic jags and shifts. Between the frozen waves and the limestone cliff, a narrow trail of rocks and pebbles opens.

J scans the field behind us as though he's dropped something valuable in the clots of scrub grass and ice chunks wide as Jersey barriers. The pebbles under our boots contain an abundance of fossils. I pocket one bone the length of my finger, warn smooth, and rub its osseous tissue until it absorbs the heat of my thumb. J folds the map. Black cirrus strafes the flat blue sky over the smallness of our bodies, our negligible footprints. Whether or not we exist has little to do with our will to exist or with the emotions that blur us. Our existence is contingent, subject to detour, buoyed by people and incongruous objects.

Water seeps from the cliff face. The brine electrifies my hair. I can't know exactly the moment at which I, too, will become permeable; I can't hear its whisper; I hear only the wind's incomprehensible drawl. I try to decipher the feeling: its alphabet of faiths: that language will unveil itself; that a person will make themselves recognizable; that desire, if true, can be transferred from the tyranny of wishing to the creation of beautiful works; that I love you without knowing you or naming you; that a landscape will reciprocate with attention and patience and practice.

8.8

An origin story: As a child in New England, I followed stone walls deep into the woods where wood stoves, crumbled chimneys, and rusted appliances lay in clearings among the pines, oaks, and maples, as though the walls of houses had simply vanished, leaving their hearths intact but exposed to sky. I imagined this was what happened to houses when families moved on from them: the foundation of my affinity for the neglected and my ambivalence towards continuity in poetic form.

S and I played among the rubbish. As the area developed, someone collected the trash; the trees were felled, stumps scraped, to bald the hills as McMansions soared into landscaped estate cul-de-sacs named Hamptons Ridge, Eagle Crest, Silver Dollar Landing.

The McMansions were all-threshold. Stand before the front door of a McMansion, then retreat to the street: from a 90-degree angle street view, the McMansion will appear depthless. For the passerby, the McMansion is a backdrop.

The entrances of Frederic Jameson's Los Angeles Westin, its sky blue cylindrical vessels, are obscure: The hotel is camouflaged volume, no door. Approaching the McMansion obliquely, as one would while passing anonymously in a car, one is seized by its conspicuous volume, incongruous with nature. For the invited visitor approaching the front atrium on foot, the McMansion is flat: all windows, all door.

How thirsty we are to offer a threshold into a superior experience.

How thirsty we are to enter into our manipulated perspectives, our fabrications.

8.9

An origin story: I stand at the threshold of the burnt remains of the Greenpoint Terminal Market and write: "A building is an exterior that narrates the interior."

After the Aughts, I add: "Tell me this in a language that I can understand."

Thirsty for sincerity, theory and irony grow self-conscious.

Hold my hand.

9.1

The closer I get to myself, the less I rely on theory.

I open a door. *Follow me.*

9.2

Once, we lived in a house
with many entrances, no exits.
There was no reason to leave,
no will to slip out. To sleep, to read
a book, to doze on the couch,
to cook in the fine blue dish, to toss
or mix in the clear blue bowl
was everything. Dawn rolled down the hill

and dusk crept up it. Only once,
I stood at the porch screen
on a snowy winter night and felt
the end enter me. And then, it was only
a chill. I spread birdseed
on the ice for the cardinal
that mocked every bedroom
window and the chickadees
that slit the dry shrubs with laughter,
their hee-hee-hee and the black bear came
on flat feet and licked it up the way
I used to lick my Laffy Taffy. The world
is a baby. Once, I climbed the tallest
evergreen to see if I could see
the neighboring town. I fell.
Its lowest branches caught me.
The real end will be
like this. Like driving through nebulae
of moths, or frogs with the summer's fat
rain sizzling on the asphalt and I love you
like a cracked egg.
I love you like a raw paw.
I love you like a city
no one can afford
after the last register's
been cleaned out, the last mop's
been slapped in the slop bucket.
I love you like green pennies
and the sunburned palms of maples.

I love you like the 4th of July
we sat barefoot on the hill
to watch the fire show. How
many entrances. How
many doors. How
I would look and look
and see and see. Dawn
slides down the green grass. Dusk
sprints up it. I love you
like the fine blue ceramic I never got clean
because I used it to roast a chicken.
I love you
like the storm that cracks
open like a bead curtain. I love you
when I climb the flagpole
to see how far I can see
in this city no one can afford. I fall.
You catch me.

9.3

In the Aughts, I read Masha Tupitsyn's *Beauty Talk and Monsters*. Her mother, an academic, patiently explained film and its ideologies to her little girl.

My mother and I watched movies, too, but my mother didn't speak of theory. Movie watching was simple: We looked in the same direction. *Triadic joint attention.* We established a common reference, followed a predetermined narrative and stuck with it for a period of time, even if the ending was anticlimactic or a total bummer, even if it unexpectedly roped us into a sequel. We knew the end would come, but knowing didn't sour the experience. Watching a movie with another person is a definition of love.

9.4

Love didn't spare me from a movie's questions. I wanted to know why some characters lived, why some had to die. I wanted to know why villains spoke with German accents until they spoke Chinese. I wanted to know why actresses looked like other actresses. I wanted to know why there must always be a loss before the protagonist is issued integrity, identity, self-worth, a place to sleep.

9.5

One thing I admired about the man I mistakenly loved was how he spent every 4th of July fishing with his father. No parties, no fireworks, just water, his father, and whatever swam to them. It was a kind of freedom for him.

I didn't care for Hemingway, but I cared for this: the human urge to establish meaningful personal ritual in the wake of the commercialized, communal ritual of capital. This is also a definition of love, a definition of family.

9.6

Almost a decade later, I returned to the Baltic Klint in the summer months. I followed an asphalt path skirted by a chain link fence to the water's one point of access. The *Aries* remained moored at its station. The pebbles were gone. The ice path that J and I had followed along the base of the cliff had melted into the black brine that slapped against the escarpment. I surveyed the sediment at the tide line: no bones. The open land where we once dipped between troughs of snow to a bombed-out circle of rebar and concrete was gated and guarded. Europe had arrived with its Euro and its clean, mobile technologies. The Pakri Peninsula would soon be host to white windmills, their aerodynamic blades snapping shadows across the once blighted fields. The economic struggle that had been visible early in the decade had been cleared from view.

9.7

An origin story: I am a little girl and I am standing on the deck of our red house overlooking the lake. It is our last day in the red house. I am holding my mother's camera, peering through the viewfinder, engrossed in a world that has become suddenly formal.

In this memory, which increases in its tenacity and in its isolation (I can't remember the moment that preceded it or the moment that followed), I have fixed the viewfinder on a bunch of marigolds in a clay pot. White and gold marigolds. As though I'd been looking for them. My whole life, searching for marigolds.

And in the white knuckle of the largest and most central flower, a black and yellow bumblebee. I fix the bumblebee in my focus, though I cannot remember if I take its picture. I think not, because a photograph never surfaces, and because logic dictates that my mother must have asked me to hold the camera but not to use it. Film was expensive. We were moving out of the red house because she couldn't afford to heat it. Photograph or no photograph, at the moment I fix my view on the bee, the photograph, however probable, however possible, has already become redundant. The bee on the flower is enough.

I am irretrievably fixed in its moment: The moment at which I first feel the emergence of memory. I stand on a precipice: I know that what I am seeing will flee. I know that I must be careful. I know, dressed in a green smocking dress with white pinafore, that if I don't perform memory's labor, I will forget. I am new to forgetting. I have already forgotten. Already its tragedy blooms in me. I watch the bee labor to extract nutrients from the flower and I will remember.

Mother, I promise I will remember. I will remember the unbelievable marigold and the plump impossibility of the bee. I will remember its puny wingspan, its corpulent body, its low and supple flight. The bee is important. It carries a code I haven't yet been schooled to unlock. All I know is I am changed. My mother collects her camera, takes my hand, locks the empty house, and I begin the long rehearsal I know I will require to keep the bee and its marigold with me in this world, and me in theirs.

9.8

To some, the ruins of industry, the ruins of the military industrial complex, are eyesores; to some, they are ancient ritual grounds, spirit gateways; to some, they are ground zero a trail to blaze. For developers, they are pure potential: liberated land, a golden capsule of airspace. Some ruins become artist residencies, state parks, and national monuments. Regardless of their forward trajectories, the dominant quality of our industrial and modern centuries' ruins is that they are *seen with intensity*. They are consequence made legible, tangible, global loss on a human scale. And as their detritus disappears as their rinds and cores are, groomed for wind farms and public parks, rezoned for condominiums with helipads and valet garages, I can only say: I breathed their capsized air. The centuries they embody are undeniable. When we agree to forget, we free ourselves of the past. What comes next is, by definition, uncertain.

9.9

When I look back on myself as a girl in the Aughts, I see a kite. A plump and colorful kite, not the most expensive or the most creatively shaped. There are other kites on the beach. Where the sand narrows, there is the danger of becoming tangled in other kite strings. The more advanced models have three or four tethers: a team directs their arabesques like puppeteers maneuvering marionettes. My kite is unexceptional, though its ostentatious print, a print designed to reference an earlier decade's paint splash typography, lends its wingspan the illusion of generosity. The kite isn't capable of harnessing enough lift to throw a person into the air or drag them into the ocean, though the kite lacks nothing: It has the requisite components: wood frame, nylon wings, string long enough to reach the hand that guides it, a hand of which it remains oblivious. On a clear day, my kite rises and cruises on the breeze like a tractor-trailer on an interstate. Its ambition is to gain as much altitude as possible while remaining loyal to the land. In turbulence, the kite is passive. It doesn't act; it reacts. This is one shortcoming of many. It tugs at its reins as though its lust for forward motion weren't merely a consequence of forces, as though its stasis weren't merely tension between the string, the nylon, the frame, and the wind's infinite jets. The kite is bound by its structural limits and by the limits of the day, bookended by the sun's twin deliveries. It's in a sudden gust that the kite is most aware of its internal tension, its snapping point. The kite doesn't break. I realize how strong its string is: strong as a spider's web: strong, but relatively. The kite clips but it does not capsize. The kite, like the present, remains.

10

A Song

> All day I've intended
> but the hills insist
>
> the destination
> resembles a sun
>
> and we will too
> someday
>
> No night is ever
> too long
>
> No field
> too humid
>
> to stop and breathe
> what
>
> paper carries
>
> > Refrain:
>
> The world is known
> to never refuse

a word
its destination

The hills are known
to never refuse

a world its sun

SNOW

VIVID WHITE SPACE

In which a pile of snow rises to the white sky: It reaches for its soul.

My love, my labor is to pronounce, transmit its depth as the sun sets on the satellite dish. I write a book of snow; it opens itself.

Snow is designed for grandeur; it propagates its destiny by bedazzling its coat.

Snow is designed for posterity; it fortifies its enterprise by educating the exposed.

Language, having achieved complete mobility, crosses gaps and streams and walls, like snow.

I know this snow: It smells of clover. It is a form of marrow. It is inside us like lichen in a mine. Carried in song from century to century, it achieves both peace and power in one exalted lifeline.

Snow in a forest is the quilt stitched over History.

Snow on a city street is an anecdote.

The pious parking lot snow is closed; it accumulates infinities within its bounds like an inexhaustible poetic theme.

Silently, snow flies through me. I, who long for snow, look outside myself.

ON A CLEAR DAY

The light in me is the light in you and tonight that light is a cop on fire.

What I want most is for you to surrender to my world.

If I see you, does that mean I love you? Is love less a feeling and more an enhanced perception?

A nightmare: I feed my house key to my dog, who swallows it willingly.

You are everywhere and nowhere. A dad tells his son as he walks him home from Little League: *That's the nature of the pitch*, and I think he's you, but he's not. You would never wear those baggy khakis and that blue shirt two sizes too big. You aren't like that. You fit.

I remember my dream and I can't stop revising.

The world I offer. I have an urgent, compelling need to revise it. Sometimes I feel alone in suffering revision's constancy. I wonder if you can perceive it. Or if you only think I've lived in too many neighborhoods, too many apartments.

A thought I've had every day for the past five years: the CNN livestream of Occupy Oakland that went dead mid-air. The yellow tear gas and black helicopters and how, once the news stopped rolling, I searched the Occupy hashtags on Instagram and scrolled through the feed. How I lay in bed, refreshing the screen.

If thoughts are things, why can't I wring them like a washcloth or bin them with the recycling. It rained; the stoop is slippery. Get out.

There is no ideal newsfeed. On a good day, I read two newspapers before the end of the afternoon. On a bad day, I scroll the algorithms like a nervous tic. When will I be satisfied with what I've read, what I'm becoming?

I once broke up with a man who later told me in an urgent phone call that he was seeing me everywhere. *Every time I look in the rear view mirror, I see your silver car,* he told me. *Well, maybe I'm following you,* I said. I tried to be funny. He broke into tears.

Funny doesn't cut it. There is no home base. Play ball.

Optimal stopping tells me that if I don't feel satisfied by the time I've read 37% of the content, then I should stop reading directly after I experience any feeling resembling satisfaction. If I haven't yet felt it, it doesn't mean I won't feel it. It only means I must redefine satisfaction to manage my expectations.

Adapt, adapt, adapt! shouted my old gym teacher as she sparred with me. In a parent-teacher conference, she told my mother I had weak shoulders but I could be great if I learned to manage myself.

The accumulation of your variations leads me to a clearing in the forest.

I want to describe its trees to you. I blame poetry. I stare into the diffuse sheaths and witness the immeasurable dates and plans. When the environment changes, I change environments. I perform the miracle of drawing a consistent hand.

My laryngitis is psychosomatic.

Talk back is sacred.

I love my mistakes. My mistakes are proof of my ideals. They make me aware of the core continuity that strikes through me like a trunk of light.

My grandfather read three newspapers. Who am I?

I want to be kind. I want to perform small and large acts of kindness for you here and away, and not too far away. My place is to touch the world softly with whatever comes out of my mouth. Why can't I be softer. Why can't I hold you. How will I learn to be soft?

Afloat in the archipelago of real estate, in the austere apartness of office, he is a different man. The eye is a recorder; it replays his embellished fact.

Comfort no longer exists outside of power. There is no safe space, nor is there its inverse, the quarantine; there is only the illusion of boundaries. I am compelled to talk back, if only because talk back breaks the illusion of boundaries.

Refugees cross nations; Zika virus transverses states. *What am I saying. What am I really saying. What am I am really, really saying.*

The boundary of a question is a violent body.

The rain will evaporate if you ask it to.

To find the cat, we must become the cat, says the little girl crawling on the sidewalk. I can't crawl outside of culture; I can only sit on my stoop and watch the neighborhood kids bounce a rubber ball.

A culture is an aspirational world. Culture provides a frame for us to stretch our canvas. The painting is what we do with us.

I've thought about Sandra Bland every day for a year. I want to suggest she should be made a saint, but I wouldn't want to taint her pure mouth with ideology.

I think of volume as a measure of a religion's threat. A quiet religion is collective, benign. A loud religion, like Waco or fundamentalist Islam, enforces difference with a shrill noise.

Is conservatism the new anarchy?

Nostalgic for smoking, revulsed by damp butts and cigarette smoke, I daydream of server farms on remote concrete islands. What would I remember if I were stranded there? What stories would I tell around its digital fire?

The economy, too, is a collection of stories. Money is metal; money is paper; money is plastic. Our metaphoric world revises itself.

True: A body has a cost.

False: Your wealth trickles down when we touch.

A nightmare: Between sheets of drywall in an unfinished basement, I confess to him: *I wish I hadn't been so afraid.*

We built a system that shapes and is shaped by the system that shaped it. Our regulated objects are tethered to contexts. What would we build if we weren't afraid?

In the late night illucidity of incumbent sleep, I write five beautiful sentences:

Against the window, the translucent-winged moths reciprocate.
The streetlamp's downward gaze connotes a fondness for the earth.
New lofts infuse the night with a crystal's austerity.
I love what he does to my brain: He ravages my perception.
His careful suit epitomizes an orderly explanation of a disaster nearly spent.

The world is a deeply personal place. What a triumph and a horror to refine its immensities into data.

He didn't complete the crossword, though he could have. This, the mercy of mastery.

I report directly to the Executive Director. She calls me into her office to tell me I'm arrogant. I tell her I'll take it as a compliment.

In a late scene, he gives me a notebook emblazoned with undersea flora. His recognition of the small, scribbling portion of me contradicts my deep-seated belief in my own eraseability: If he can see me, can I enter History?

In an early scene, a gun is introduced with the weight of a character. It glows in the bones of the audience. We can't excuse it until it has spoken. We've burdened our objects with souls.

For a moment, I thought he couldn't love me because we didn't have the same nose. As though his silhouette in passing car light could like tea leaves read a doomed affection. To idealize him for such a reason could be dismissed as superficial, but the nose connotes as his wire-rimmed glasses, their pretense of scientific precision, scalpel-esque, imply he will parse what undresses itself with exegetical intensity. And the bliss of the finely perceived, its extreme consciousness, its newness against itself, its eventual withdrawal into itself is practically an argument for an object-oriented philosophy.

I bumbled immanence.

I'm a girl supported by the ballast of a moment.

I will never forget you because I have written you down.

Long after the last bus came and went, we walked along the Jersey barriers from Jersey City to Hoboken. He said we had an affinity. What likeness, other than a refusal, a shared lust for the smell of sawdust, a long view down the turnpike, a gaze away from futility?

The moment we love, we can no longer copy.

A love's omnipresence isn't repetition, it's a seed that sprouts where acknowledged. It reminds us that our shared habitat is the cosmic.

I want to know the geology of the paper, how far back the ink can be traced.

Stay with me here. Stay with me on the screen where nothing happens.

An atmosphere worthy of being recorded, which is to say, an atmosphere worthy of love.

BIBLIOGRAPHY

Abramović, Marina. "Deeper and Deeper: Interview with Marina Abramović." Interview by Janet
    A. Kaplan. *Art Journal*.

Agamben, Giorgio. *Remnants of Auchwitz: The Witness and the Archive*.

Apollinaire, Guillaume. *Apollinaire: Selected Poems*. Translated by Oliver Bernard.

Aristotle. *Meteorologica*.

Artaud, Antonin. *An Antonin Artaud Anthology*. Jack Hirschman, editor.

Attali, Jacques. *Noise*.

Ballard, J.G. *The Atrocity Exhibition*.

Basinski, William. *Disintegration Loops*.

Baudelaire, Charles. *The Flowers of Evil*.

Bradbury, Ray. *The Stories of Ray Bradbury*.

Brathwaite, Fred. "Change the Beat."

Butler, Judith. "The Body You Want." Interview by Liz Kotz. *Artforum*.

Cain, Ben. "Volumes for Sound." *Sound Spill*.

Celan, Paul. *Selected Poems and Prose of Paul Celan*.

Chandler, Adam. "A Warehouse Fire of Digital Memories." *The Atlantic*.

The Conqueror. Dir. Dick Powell. CinemaScope, 1956.

Deleuze, Gilles. *Difference & Repetition*.

Deleuze, Gilles. *Francis Bacon*.

Deleuze, Gilles. *What Is Philosophy?*

Dickinson, Emily. "My Life had stood – a Loaded Gun (764)."

Didion, Joan. "At the Dam." *The White Album*.

Hancock, Herbie. "Rockit."

Haraway, Donna. "A Cyborg Manifesto."

The Holy Bible, New King James Version.

Holzer, Jenny. *Truisms*.

Homer. *The Odyssey*.

Joyce, James. *Ulysses*.

Jurado, Damian. "Like Titanic."

Kakutani, Michiko. "Bending the Truth in A Million Little Ways." In *The New York Times*.

Keats, John. "Ode on a Grecian Urn."

Kilivris, Michael. "Beyond Goods and Services: Toward a Nietzschean Critique of Capitalism."

Klein, Yves. *1928–1962: Selected Writings*.

Klein, Yves. *Leap into the Void*.

Koestenbaum, Wayne. *Humiliation*.

Koestenbaum, Wayne. *My 1980s*.

Lerner, Ben. *The Lichtenburg Figures.*

Manguso, Sarah. *The Captain Lands in Paradise.*

Marker, Chris. *La Jetée.*

McCarthy, Cormac. *The Road.*

McLuhan, Marshall. *Understanding Media.*

Minkowski, Eugène. Translated by Deborah Bouchette. *Vers une cosmologie: Fragments philosophiques.*

Nietzsche, Friedrich. *The Gay Science.*

Nietzsche, Friedrich. *Twilight of the Idols, or, How to Philosophize with a Hammer.*

O'Hara, Frank. *"[Statement for the New American Poetry.]"*

Pessoa, Fernando. *The Book of Disquiet.*

Plath, Sylvia. "Lady Lazarus."

Postman, Neil. *Amusing Ourselves to Death.*

Pound, Ezra. "In A Station of the Metro."

Raleigh, Ben, Winfeld Scott and Otis Blackwell. "Don't Want Your Love Letters."

Raleigh, Ben, Winfeld Scott and Otis Blackwell. "(Return To Sender) Don't Want Your Letters."

Reines, Ariana. *Mercury.*

Rilke, Rainer Maria. *Letters to a Young Poet.*

Ruefle, Mary. *Madness, Rack, & Honey.*

Sandburg, Carl. "Among the Red Guns."

Sandburg, Carl. "A Revolver."

Scott, Winfield and Otis Blackwell. "Return to Sender."

Solomon, Andrew. "The Reckoning." In *The New Yorker.*

Solnit, Rebecca. *Savage Dreams.*

Sontag, Susan. "An Argument About Beauty."

Stevens, Sufjan. "For the Widows in Paradise, For the Fatherless in Ypsilanti."

Stevens, Wallace. "Thirteen Ways of Looking at a Blackbird."

Tupitsyn, Masha. *Beauty Talk and Monsters.*

The Qu-ran. Abu Dawood Book 32, Hadith #4090.

Von Trier, Lars. "Nymphomaniac."

Wikipedia. *Dynamo (disambiguation).*

Williams, William Carlos. "Paterson."

Zain, C.C. *The Brotherhood of Light: Divination.*

Žižek, Slavoj. *Looking Awry: An Introduction to Jacques Lacan through Popular Culture.*

Žižek, Slavoj. *The Pervert's Guide to Cinema.*

ABOUT THE AUTHOR

JASMINE DREAME WAGNER is an American poet, artist, and musician. She is the author of *Rings* (Kelsey Street Press) and five chapbooks: *Ask* (Slope Editions), *Listening for Earthquakes* (Caketrain), *Rewilding* (Ahsahta Press), *Seven Sunsets* (The Lettered Streets Press), *The Stag* (Dancing Girl Press) and an e-chapbook, *True Crime* (NAP). Her writing has appeared or is forthcoming in *American Letters & Commentary*, *Blackbird*, *Colorado Review*, *Fence*, *Guernica*, *Hyperallergic*, *New American Writing*, *Seattle Review*, *Verse*, and in two anthologies: *The Arcadia Project: North American Postmodern Pastoral* (Ahsahta Press) and *Lost and Found: Stories from New York* (Mr. Beller's Neighborhood Books).

As a singer-songwriter and multi-instrumentalist, Wagner has performed at the CMJ Music Marathon, free103point9 Wave Farm, and the Olympia Experimental Music Festival. Her multidisciplinary work in sound, text, and performance has earned her grants and residencies from the Foundation for Contemporary Arts, Hall Farm Center for Arts & Education, and The Wassaic Project. In 2013, she was awarded an Artist Fellowship from the Connecticut Office of the Arts.

AHSAHTA PRESS

NEW SERIES

AHSAHTA PRESS

SAWTOOTH POETRY PRIZE SERIES

This book is set in Apollo MT type with DIN titles
by Ahsahta Press at Boise State University.
Cover design by Quemadura.
Book design by Janet Holmes.

AHSAHTA PRESS

2017

JANET HOLMES, DIRECTOR

PATRICIA BOWEN, *intern*

SAM CAMPBELL

KATHRYN JENSEN

COLIN JOHNSON

DAN LAU

MATT NAPLES